W9-AUZ-103

A·B·C 1·2·3 CRAFT BOOK

Make a Cloth Book of Exciting Learning Toys

Phyllis Fiarotta
& Noel Fiarotta

STERLING PUBLISHING CO., INC. NEW YORK

Edited by Jeanette Green
Photography by Jerry Palubniak

Library of Congress Cataloging-in-Publication Data
Fiarotta, Phyllis.
  A-B-C 1-2-3 craft book : make a cloth book of exciting learning
toys / Phyllis Fiarotta & Noel Fiarotta.
      p.   cm.
  Includes index.
  ISBN 0-8069-0671-5
    1. Soft toy making.   2. Toy and moveable books.   3. Educational
toys.   I. Fiarotta, Noel.   II. Title.   III. Title: ABC 123 craft
book.   IV. Title: A-B-C one-two-three craft book.
TT174.3.F53   1994
745.592′4—dc20   93—40989
                                                                  CIP

2   4   6   8   10   9   7   5   3   1

Published by Sterling Publishing Company, Inc.
387 Park Avenue South, New York, N.Y. 10016
© 1994 by Phyllis Fiarotta and Noel Fiarotta
Distributed in Canada by Sterling Publishing
% Canadian Manda Group, P.O. Box 920, Station U
Toronto, Ontario, Canada M8Z 5P9
Distributed in Great Britain and Europe by Cassell PLC
Villiers House, 41/47 Strand, London WC2N 5JE, England
Distributed in Australia by Capricorn Link (Australia) Pty Ltd.
P.O. Box 6651, Baulkham Hills, Business Centre, NSW 2153,
Australia
Manufactured in the United States of America
All rights reserved

Sterling ISBN 0-8069-0671-5

Dedicated to the memory of Kelly Curtis
for her beauty, good humor, and strength

Night

CONTENTS

A·B·C 1·2·3 BASICS

The *A·B·C 1·2·3 Craft Book* transforms letters and numbers into exploration of the world in early learning. With two soft action books and many simple stuffed toys, adults and children can have hours of creative play.

Inside you'll find instructions for creating each letter and number, topics for discussion, and things to do. Some topics to interest children include lists of examples, others encourage visits to a museum, library, zoo, or walks around the neighborhood, on the beach, or in the woods. Don't feel insecure if you think "I'm not an artist." Your apple and butterfly need not look exactly like those in the book. They will be uniquely yours. That's the fun part.

When you assemble the books, be sure to keep in mind the age and aggressiveness of the child, especially when securing appliqués, buttons, and decorative spangles. Always stress gentle handling to minimize wear and maximize safety. Also, be sure to consider what is age appropriate for the child.

With the first page of *My ABCs* and *123,* children can begin a journey of discovery through curiosity, creativity, and learning.

Fabric

We made the letter and the number pages shown in these book pages on standard-size felt pieces. The appliqués are also felt. You can also make a book in washable cotton or cotton blend, but because felt is durable and easy to handle, it's the fabric we recommend.

Craft Felt—Felt is a sturdy nonwoven fabric that is available in synthetic and wool blends. It's sold by the piece or by the yard. The standard piece is roughly 9 × 12 inches (22.5 × 30 cm), although dimensions vary slightly with each manufacturer. Because most stores carry a limited selection of felt and manufacturers produce different color ranges, collect a variety of colors from several outlets.

Woven Fabric—Use washable cotton or cotton blends in solids and prints.

Designing the Book

The standard felt piece is an ideal book size. Depending on the price, however, felt by the yard can be more economical. This is especially true for a book made smaller or larger than the standard piece size. But it's easy to calculate how much felt or fabric to buy. Use this information for your calculations:

Number of Pages—The total number of pages includes a front and a back cover. The contents of a book can include:

- The complete alphabet or numbers 0 to 9
- Selected letters and/or numbers
- Words or names (without pictures), using the designs of the letter toys
- A mix of pictures and letters

Page Color and Size—Choose light tones and white. Trim pages to the same size.

Appliqués—Buy a wide selection of colors for the appliqués.

Felt Tabs—Every two pages have a felt tab that's 2 inches (10 cm) wide and the height of the book, for binding. Tabs can be white or in a variety of colors.

Patterns

Typing paper is an ideal weight and size for patterns. You can also use brown paper bags. Small decorative details, such as designs in butterfly wings, may be cut freehand directly from fabric. Always try to cut sharp, even edges. Since most designs are simple, you can easily draw them freehand. This includes some designs placed on grids.

Freehand Patterns—All appliqué designs can be drawn freehand.

Partly Freehand Patterns—Some appliqué designs can be placed inside specific-size squares and rectangles.

Draw freehand designs within the specific measurements.

Tracing—Each project begins with a capital and lowercase letter or with a number. Trace each letter or number on lightweight paper or tracing paper for your patterns. You can draw them freehand, if you like.

Grids—Some patterns are placed on grids—networks of squares with specific measurements. On the grid shown, 1 square equals 1 inch or 2.5 cm. For all grids:

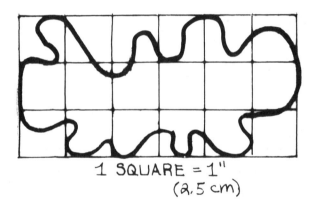

1 SQUARE = 1"
(2.5 cm)

1. Count the number of boxes of the grid across and down.

2. Using a pencil and a ruler, duplicate the same number of boxes across and down on paper. Draw the lines parallel, 1 inch (2.5 cm) apart from each other, creating a network of 1-inch (2.5-cm) boxes.

3. Study how the free-form shape passes from box to box, as it cuts corners, curves diagonally across, and follows grid lines. Duplicate the design on your enlarged grid.

Constructing the Pages

Generally, the designs fill the bottom two-thirds of the alphabet and number pages, with their identifying letters and words in the upper third. In the sewing instructions, we refer to the design elements as appliqués.

Thread—Although thread can match the color of each appliqué, using a neutral or invisible thread throughout avoids changing spools and bobbins.

Layering—Sew smaller appliqués to larger appliqués before pinning them in place on their intended pages.

Top Stitching—Because felt is non-woven, raw edges do not need to be turned under. Machine or hand-stitch appliqués in place, 1/8 to 1/4 inch (.31 to .62 cm) in from all edges. For fabric appliqués, sew a zigzag stitch over the raw edges, or hand stitch, turning the raw edges under.

Sewing Shortcuts—Stitching can be minimized in many cases. For example, here are some shortcuts for the dragon on pages 27–28:

- Stitch the arm to the body along the top, straight edge, leaving the arm free to move.

- Sew a single stitch line along the dragon's back, eliminating the need to sew along the zigzag edge.

- Sew the grass on three sides, allowing the blades to stand free.

Circles—Round appliqués, such as eyes and the sun, can be sewn in place with two or more crisscrossing lines, creating added detail.

Double Stitching—To secure the stitching, double stitch first and last stitches.

Ironing—After all appliqués are sewn in place, steam press flat each completed page on the wrong (back) side.

Finishing—Trim away all hanging threads.

Appliqués

FIXED APPLIQUÉS
Fixed or stationary appliqués are sewn directly to the page.

MOVEABLE APPLIQUÉS
Moveable appliqués are double-sided and attached to the designs with buttons. Some have limited movement, others free movement. For safety, be sure to attach the button securely. Adding a lightweight plastic backing (freezer bags are good), cut to shape, gives the appliqué smoother movement.

Cutting—Cut out two identical shapes for each moveable appliqué.

Decorations—Sew or glue any felt and spangle details to one shape. Make sure everything is safe and secure for the age of the child.

Self-Fastening Tape— Buy tape economically by the yard. Cut tape into 1/4- to 1/2-inch (.62- to 1.25-cm) squares. Use strips for larger appliqués. Sew tape to appropriate places. Reinforce stitching.

Assembly—Sew the shapes together, right side facing out, ⅛ inch (.31 cm) from the edges. For a perfect match, sew a shape to a piece of uncut felt and trim away the excess.

Limited Movement Appliqués—(see illustration)

• Place the appliqué on the design.
• Place a button on the appliqué at the attachment point.
• Attach in place by sewing many stitches through the button and all layers. (Make sure it's "child-proof.") Secure the button at the back of the page with multiple stitches.
• Add a dab of glue to the stitches both on the button and on the back of the page for added security.

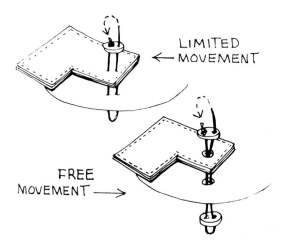

LIMITED
← MOVEMENT

FREE
MOVEMENT →

Free Movement Appliqués (see illustration)—Follow the same directions for attaching limited movement appliqués. However, you'll need to sew a second button at the back of the page. The stitches will pass through a common hole, which can be made by twisting the point of some scissors through all fabric layers.

INDEPENDENT APPLIQUÉS
You can slip independent appliqués into pockets, attach them with yarn, or adhere them to the page with self-fastening tape. Avoid using very small, loose pieces with very young children.

Cutting—Cut two matching shapes.

Decorations—Sew or glue felt and spangle details to the shape.

Self-Fastening Tape—Sew one half of the self-fastening tape to the center of the other shape with crisscrossing lines. Sew the matching half to its corresponding place on the page.

Assembly—Sew the two shapes together, right sides facing out, ⅛ inch (.31 cm) from the edges. For a perfect match, sew a shape to a piece of uncut felt and trim away the excess.

Embellishments

Be creative with trimmings and spangles, available at craft counters and stores. But keep in mind the age of the child and safety concerns.

Glued-on Appliqués—Tiny felt appliqués, such as eyes and highlights, can be glued in place. Tacky glue dries strong, flexible, and clear. Immediately wipe away excess glue from the fabric with a wet sponge. You can use a glue gun, if you like. Allow the glue to dry completely.

Hand Embroidery—Embroider decorative details and identifying words on the page with an array of stitches.

Machine Stitching—Add machine-stitched details to designs or backgrounds.

Spangles—Sew large craft sequins and other spangles securely in place. Only use these if the child is old enough not to remove or eat them. Add a drop of glue to the stitches for added security. For unsewn sequins, add a large drop of tacky glue to their concave sides and press them firmly onto the fabric, forcing a bead of glue through the center hole.

Yarn—Knitting yarn, sewn or glued on, can create thick lines, such as a flower stem or a happy smile.

Trimmings—Add finishing touches with ribbon, gathered lace, rickrack, ball fringe, embroidered patches, and other things that strike your fancy and that may be sewn securely to the page.

Fabric Paints

Use fabric paints, sold in plastic bottles in bright and iridescent colors, for words and decorative details.

Paint Test—Practise controlling the flow and thickness of the line on paper, then on a scrap of the intended fabric.

Raised Fibers—Some felt has raised fibers which catch on the paint. Cut them away with scissors on the area to be painted.

Lettering Guide—Lay two parallel, dark-colored threads on the area you want to letter. Carefully print letters between but not touching the guide lines. Carefully remove the threads.

Drying—Depending on the thickness of the applied paint, drying time can be up to eight hours. It's best to dry the fabric overnight. Avoid smudging.

Ironing—Never use a hot iron directly on fabric paint. If you must iron a completed page that has fabric paint on it, turn the page over and iron on the wrong side. Caution: synthetic blends can melt with a hot iron.

Highlights—Add white or pearl highlights and grey shadows for added dimension.

Decorative Details—Be creative.

Letter Toys

Each project includes instructions for making a soft letter or number toy, which duplicates its book counterpart. The same sewing and assembly procedures apply, with the addition of a layer of stuffing (Fiberfil or batting). The size can vary from tiny to jumbo.

Assembling the Book

Whether your intended book will include a few letter or number pages or the entire alphabet, you can assemble pages like those in a loose-leaf binder.

Interfacing—Pages made of cotton or cotton blends may require extra body. Consider sewing every two pages together with a lightweight interfacing, cut to size, between them.

Tabs—Both felt and cotton books require felt tabs for binding. You can use oil cloth or vinyl. For every two pages, cut one tab measuring 2 inches (10 cm) wide and as long as the height of the book.

Sewing—Machine or hand embroider pages together with ¼-inch (.62-cm) seams.

For felt books, place every two pages together, with a tab inserted on the left, ½ inch (1.25 cm) in. Sew the pages together along the four sides.

For cotton or cotton blend books, pin every two pages together, right sides facing. Place the tab between the pages with all edges lined up. Pin the interfacing to the outside. Sew together along three and a half sides. Turn the pages inside out and sew the open seam closed. Press flat.

Binding Holes—Punch three equally spaced holes along the length of each tab. The holes on all tabs should be in line with each other. A paper punch works well.

Bindings—Use thick gift wrap yarn or several multi-colored lengths of knitting yarn to tie the pages together. You can also use 3-inch (7.5-cm) loose-leaf rings, sold at stationery stores.

ABC QUILT AND OTHER IDEAS

QUILT—You can eliminate the capital and small letters and words of each design from the quilt. If you want to use words, consider embroidery instead of fabric paint. Sew all moveable and independent appliqués in place as single-ply appliqués.

Designs—Select an array of designs from the alphabet and number books. You can incorporate a name or sentence, like "TOMMY SLEEPS HERE," into the overall patchwork, using the designs of the letter and number toys.

Size—Make the base square 9 inches (22.5 cm). Use a smaller square for a baby's quilt.

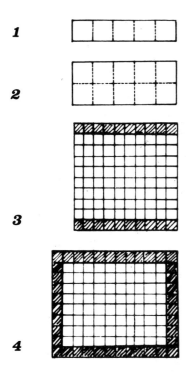

Calculation—Draw a diagram on paper with the number of appliquéd squares. Add a border of plain squares on the four sides. Calculate the amount of fabric needed.

Fabric—Choose washable cotton or cotton blends in a variety of solid colors for the base squares. Appliqués can be a mixture of solids, calicos, stripes, plaids, or what you wish.

Base Squares—Cut all squares exactly the same size.

Appliqués—Follow instructions for cutting and sewing appliqués to the base squares, described in "Constructing the Pages."

Arrangement—Arrange the designed squares in consecutive order, or mix the designs. Place some designs sideways or upside down. Consider background colors in relationship to each other.

Assembly—Sew all seams exactly ¼ inch (.62 cm).

1. Sew the top row of squares together.
2. Construct the second row and sew it to the first. Continue adding rows.
3. Sew a row of border squares to the top and bottom of the patchwork.
4. Sew a row of border squares to each side of the patchwork.

Ironing—Press the quilt on the backside. Open all seams as you press.

Fabric Paint—Add detail, if desired.

Construction—Here are some hints.

• Cut quilt batting (optional) and the quilt's backing to the size of the completed patchwork.
• Place the patchwork and the backing together, right sides facing, with the batting on top.
• Sew the layers together along three

and a half sides, ½ inch (1.25 cm) from the edges.

- Turn inside out and hand or machine stitch the open seam closed.
- To quilt, pin or baste stitch the layers together. Stitch along the seam lines or at the corners.

PLAY BOARD—With their moveable and independent appliqués, sew a patchwork of designs to form a large play board for the floor or bed.

PAPER PROJECTS—You can make all the designs in colored construction paper and use them in a classroom, daycare center, or home.

BANNER—Sew words, names, or designs to standard-size felt pieces. Sew two felt or ribbon loops to the top of each. Hang the finished banner on a pole.

POCKET ORGANIZER—Sew letter and number pages along the sides and bottoms on a felt background to create pockets for toys, crayons, and other small items.

MY ABCs BOOK COVER

Instructions

1. Draw patterns for the letters free-hand, or trace letters from their design pages.
2. Use patterns to cut letters from colored felt.
3. Make the sun with four warm-color semicircles in graduated sizes. The largest semicircle measures about 4½ × 7½ inches (11.25 × 18.75 cm). Cut them freehand or make patterns.
4. Sew or glue eyes and cheeks on the smallest semicircle. The mouth can be fabric paint or yarn.
5. Sew the semicircles together, one on top of the other, with the straight sides flush.
6. Pin the appliqués on the page and sew them in place.
7. Sew on a ribbon or trim border.

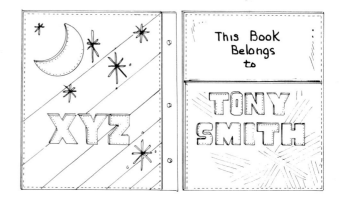

Back Cover

The back cover can be plain, or you could add an appliqué design or a large pocket to hold extra, independent appliqués.

Aa APPLE

Up·
Down·
Across

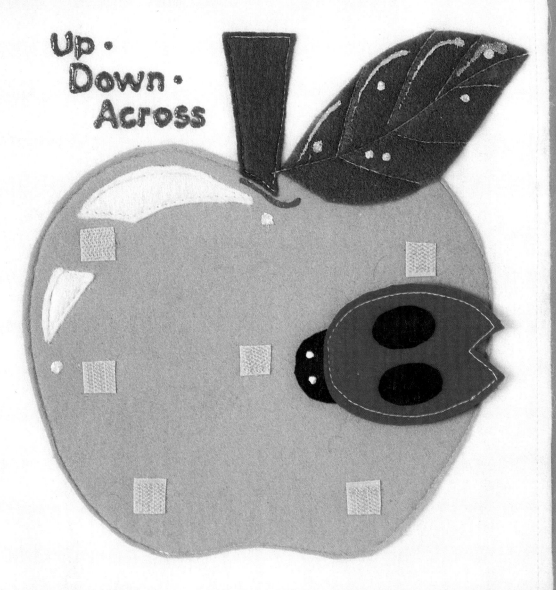

APPLE

Up, Down, Across

Move the ladybug up, down, and across the apple.

Discuss

- Things that go *up*—airplane, dandelion seed blow-ball, bird; *down*—submarine, rain, sunshine, apple from tree; *across*—train, car, boat, horizon
- Where fruit grows—on trees, vines, bushes, plants
- Apple colors—red, yellow, green, combination of colors
- Apple names—McIntosh, Granny Smith, Rome, Winesap, Delicious
- Foods made with apples—apple pie, apple butter, applesauce, apple cider

Things to Do

- Help make an apple pie.
- Make dried apple-head dolls.
- Read the story of Johnny Appleseed.
- Read the poem "Ladybug, Ladybug Fly Away."
- Make **dry apple slices.**
  1. Peel and core crisp apples.
  2. Cut apples into rings.
  3. Lay rings on paper in a sunny spot.
  4. Turn fruit often until dry—several days, depending on the amount of sun.

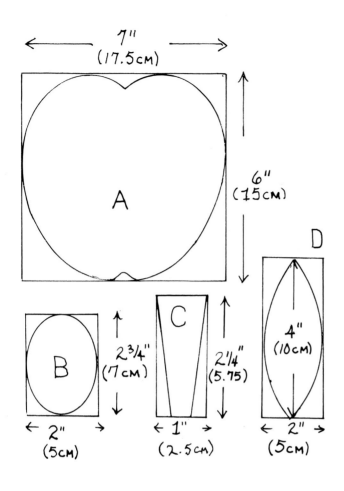

4. Pin the appliqués on the page and sew them in place.
5. Sew self-fastening tape on the apple—along the sides and in the middle.
6. Print the words "APPLE," "Up," "Down," and "Across" with fabric paint. Draw decorative details.

LETTER TOY

1. Draw a large *A* on paper for the pattern.
2. Using the pattern, cut out two felt letters.
3. Sew self-fastening tape along one letter.
4. Sew the two letters together with a little stuffing between them.
5. Make a ladybug as described above.

Instructions

LETTER PAGE

1. **Patterns**—Draw an apple (A), ladybug (B), stem (C), and leaf (D) to the dimensions shown. Trace *Aa*.
2. Using the patterns, cut appliqués from felt. Also cut out apple highlights and two ladybug shapes.
3. To construct the ladybug (see "Independent Appliqués," p. 10), sew a head and oval markings on one oval and self-fastening tape on the other before sewing the two together.

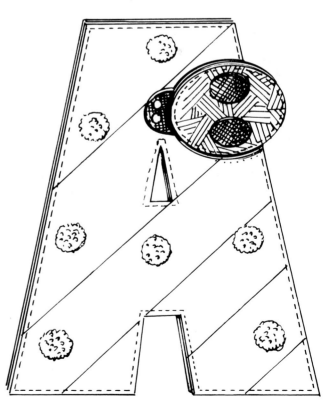

Bb

BUTTERFLY

Through

BUTTERFLY

Through

Pass the balls of the antennas through the holes in the butterfly's wings.

Discuss

- Things that pass *through* other things—sunlight through a window, thread through the eye of needle, car through a tunnel
- Differences between moths and butterflies
- How caterpillars become butterflies
- Other winged insects

Things to Do

- Make many photocopies of the outline of a butterfly for coloring.
- Discover the caterpillar in Lewis Carroll's *Alice in Wonderland.*
- Create **edible butterflies.**

On a plate, arrange two halves of a slice of bread, cut on the diagonal, for the wings and a hot dog for the body. Add mustard and ketchup designs.

On a plate, arrange two slices of melon for the wings, and strawberries, blueberries, or sliced fruit for the body.

On a dish of gelatin or pudding, arrange halved pineapple ring wings and a whipped topping body.

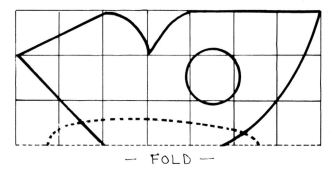

— FOLD —

1 SQUARE = 1"
(2.5 cm)

Instructions

LETTER PAGE

1. **Patterns**—Fold 6 × 7-inch (15 × 17.5-cm) paper in half and draw a butterfly wing (body will be on the fold). Draw a 1½-inch (3.75-cm) circle placed on the wing design shown. (The placement of the holes will match those of the clown's eyes on the reverse page.) If you wish, you can enlarge the designs on the grid (1 square = 1 inch or 2.5 cm). (See "Grids," p. 8.) Trace *Bb*.
2. Cut out the patterns. Leave part of the fold of the butterfly uncut. Cut out the circles.
3. Using the patterns, cut appliqués from felt. Cut out the circles on the wings. Also cut out a body and wing designs.
4. Sew wing designs to the butterfly.
5. Pin the appliqués to a page and sew them in place.
6. For the antennas, glue or sew pompoms (ball fringe) to the ends of two lengths of yarn.

7. Sew the body to the butterfly with the ends of the antennas tucked under the head.
8. Print the words "BUTTERFLY" and "Through" with fabric paints. Draw decorative details.

LETTER TOY

1. Draw a large *B* on paper for the pattern. The openings should be large enough for a pompom to pass through.
2. Using the pattern, cut out two felt letters.
3. Tuck the ends of two constructed antennas between the letters, as shown.
4. Sew the two letters together with a little stuffing between them.

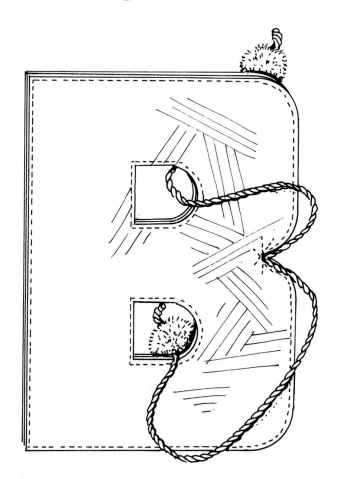

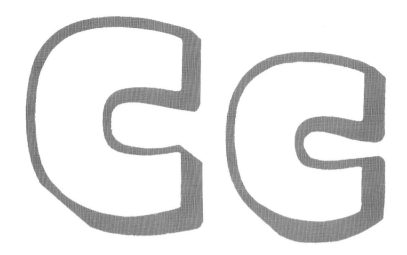

CLOWN

Happy, Sad

Turn the clown's mouth up or down to make him happy or sad.

Discuss

- Things that make people *happy*—a funny face, birthday cake, ice cream; *sad*—a rainy day, scraped knee
- Emotions—love, frustration, anger, fear, excitement
- Individual faces and costumes of clowns
- Animals that work in a circus
- Other circus performers

Things to Do

- Make many photocopies of a simple clown face (circle) and hat (triangle). Color in funny clown makeup and costumes.
- Create real clown faces on children as a rainy-day activity or at a birthday party with a circus theme. Use adult, play, costume, or Halloween makeup.
- Create **fruit clowns.**
  1. Cut large dried fruits into eyes, noses, cheeks, mouths. Prunes and raisins can be used as is.
  2. Attach features to apples, pears, peaches, or nectarines, using prepared frosting or cream cheese as an adhesive.
  3. Top with shredded coconut hair.

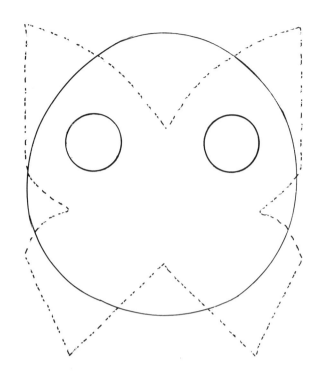

7. To construct the clown's mouth (see "Independent Appliqué," p. 10), sew self-fastening tape to one mouth shape. Sew the shapes together.
8. Print "CLOWN," "Happy," and "Sad" with fabric paints.

LETTER TOY

1. Draw a large *C* on paper for the pattern.
2. Using the pattern, cut one letter from a warm color of felt and another from a cool color.
3. Sew or glue a happy face on the warm color and a sad face, upside down, on the cool color.
4. Sew the letters together with a little stuffing between them.
5. Flip the letter to change from happy to sad.

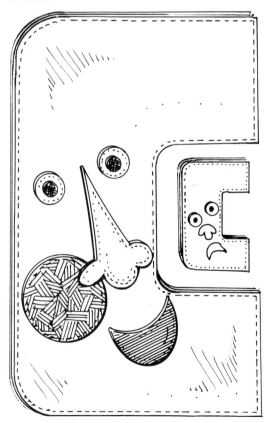

Instructions

LETTER PAGE

1. **Patterns**—Make the clown's face a 5½-inch (13.75-cm) circle. Trace *Cc*.
2. Using the patterns, cut appliqués from felt. Also cut out a nose, triangles (for above the eyes), cheeks, two smiling mouths, and hair.
3. Sew the nose, triangles, and cheeks on the face. Sew on a narrow strip of self-fastening tape where the mouth will be.
4. Pin the appliqués (except the mouth) to a page. Tuck hair under the top and a collar under the bottom of the face. Sew all appliqués in place.
5. To cut out the clown's eyes, place the butterfly page on the clown page, with designs facing out. Trace around the holes.
6. Cut out the traced holes.

DRAGON

Open, Close

Open and close the dragon's mouth to see its fiery tongue.

Discuss

- Things that *open* and *close*—door, box lid, book, mouth, hand, drawer
- Storybook dragons
- Chinese New Year dragon dance
- Dragonfly
- Mythical creatures—dragon, sea serpent, mermaid, unicorn, flying horse

Things to Do

- Roar like a dragon while opening and closing the dragon's mouth.
- Make up a scary story about a dragon.
- Create **dinodragons and dragonsaurs.**
  1. Photocopy pictures of dinosaurs.
  2. Color in wings, scales, and fiery breath.

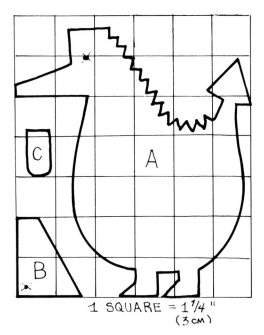

1 SQUARE = 1¼"
(3 cm)

Instructions

LETTER PAGE

1. **Patterns**—Enlarge the designs placed on the grid (1 square = 1¼ inches or 3.12 cm). (See "Grids," p. 8.)
2. Using the patterns, cut from felt the body (A), two upper heads (B), and two arms (C). Also cut out two rows of teeth, a red tongue, a flower, and grass. Trace *Dd*.
3. Sew an arm and the flower to the body.
4. Pin the appliqués (except upper head) to the page. Tuck the other arm, teeth, and the tongue under the body. Sew all appliqués in place.
5. To construct the upper head, sew an eye to one shape. Sew the shapes together with the second row of teeth tucked between them.

6. To attach the upper head, see "Moveable Appliqués," "Limited Movement," pp. 9–10.
7. Print "DRAGON," "Open," and "Close" with fabric paints. Draw decorative details. The flower stem can be yarn.

LETTER TOY

1. Draw a large *D*, without the middle opening on paper for the pattern.
2. Using the pattern, cut out two felt letters.
3. From a different color, cut two smaller *D* shapes the size of the letter's middle opening.
4. Sew a *D* shape, with an appliqué or fabric paint daisy, to the middle of a letter.
5. Sew the other *D* shape over the flowered shape, along the straight edge.
6. Sew the letters together with a little stuffing between them.

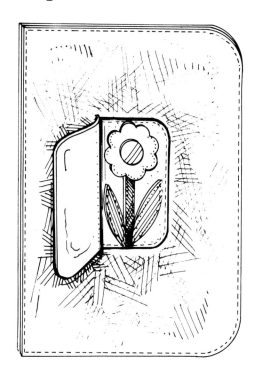

DRAGON

Open • Close

Ee EGGS

In·Out

EGGS

In, Out

Take the eggs out of the carton and put them back in.

Discuss

- Things that go *in* and *out*—books from the library, milk in the refrigerator, hands in pockets
- Animals that lay eggs—chicken, lizard, fish, frog, alligator, platypus
- Which came first, the chicken or the egg?
- Cooking eggs—scrambled, hardboiled, sunny side up, over easy, omelette
- Legend of the Easter egg
- Size and color of eggs
- "The goose that laid the golden egg" in the tale "Jack and the Beanstalk"

Things to Do

- Recite the nursery rhyme "Humpty Dumpty."
- Color and decorate eggs.
- On a rainy day or for a birthday party, arrange an egg hunt.
- Create **eggshell mosaics.**
  1. Save cracked eggshells.
  2. Dye shells in food coloring or Easter egg dyes.
  3. Break the shells into little pieces.
  4. Glue the shells to a coloring book picture.

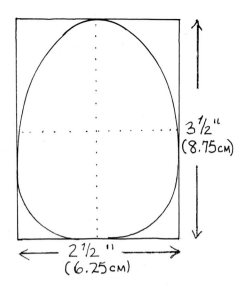

3½" (8.75cm)

2½" (6.25cm)

Instructions

LETTER PAGE

1. **Patterns**—Draw an egg to the dimensions shown. Trace *Ee*.

2. Using the patterns, cut out felt appliqués. Cut out eight eggs. Cut out two rectangles about 2¾ × 7¾ inches (6.9 × 19.4 cm). Also cut out eyes and smiling mouths.

3. Pin the letters on the page and sew them in place.

4. For the egg cartons, pin the rectangles on the page, 1 inch (2.5 cm) apart. Sew each along the bottom and halfway up the sides and middle, securing the end stitches well. Cut into the middle of each rectangle, up to the stitches.

5. Sew or glue eyes and a mouth on four ovals.

6. To construct the eggs (see "Independent Appliqués," p. 10), sew each oval with a face to a plain oval.

7. Print the words "EGGS," "In," and "Out" with fabric paint.

LETTER TOY

1. Draw a large *E* on paper for the pattern.

2. Using the pattern, cut out two felt letters.

3. Since the letter will only be stuffed on the left side, you'll need a line of stitches down the middle (see arrow). Sew each crossbar along the side and bottom, to create pockets.

4. Make eggs to fit inside the pockets as described for the letter page. Add appliqué or fabric paint faces.

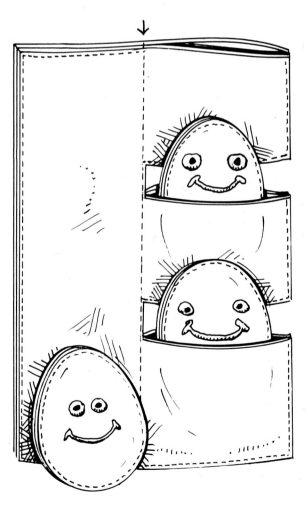

FISH

Count

Count the number of fish scales.

Discuss

- Things you *count*—numbers on a clock, eggs in a carton, fingers and toes, bananas or grapes in a bunch
- Other creatures that live in the sea— clams, jellyfish, lobsters, sea horses
- Why a whale is not a fish
- Mermaids and mermen

Things to Do

- Draw a school of fish.
- Visit a pet shop.
- Buy a goldfish to take care of.
- Here's a **go fishing game.**
  1. Cut many simple fish shapes from colored felt.
  2. Sew a small square of self-fastening tape to each fish.
  3. For a fishing pole, tie string to an unsharpened pencil. Sew self-fastening tape to the end of the string.

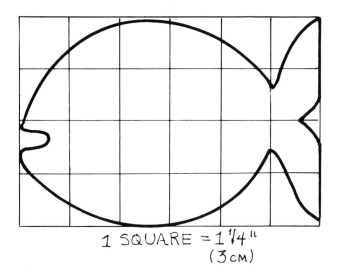

1 SQUARE = 1¼" (3 CM)

LETTER TOY

1. Draw a large *F* on paper for the pattern.
2. Using the pattern, cut out two felt letters.
3. Cut out many small felt circles in different colors.
4. Sew or glue the circles scattered on one letter.
5. Sew the letters together with a little stuffing between them.
6. Draw numbers on the circles with fabric paints.

Instructions

LETTER PAGE

1. **Patterns**—Draw a simple fish shape on a 5 × 8-inch (12.5 × 20-cm) piece of paper, or enlarge the fish on the grid (1 square = 1¼ inch or 3.12 cm). (See "Grids," p. 8.) Trace *Ff*.
2. Using the patterns, cut appliqués from felt. Also cut out six to ten fish scales, fins, and an eye.
3. Sew the fish scales to the fish, along the straight sides. Sew on the eye.
4. Pin the appliqués to a page with the fins tucked under the fish. Sew the appliqués in place.
5. Print the words "FISH" and "Count" and the numbers on the fish scales with fabric paint.
6. Add sequin and paint bubbles, as you like. The little fish is a commercial appliqué. You can create your own little fish, if you wish, or simply eliminate it.

GRASS

Behind

Part the grass to find the worm hiding behind it.

Discuss

- Things that are behind other things—wall behind a picture, backyard behind a house
- Where grass grows—front lawn, sand dunes, bamboo forests, fields
- Grasses that produce food—bamboo, corn, wheat, barley, oats
- What worms do not have that animals do—eyes, nose, arms, legs, claws

What kind of worm has eyes? A bookworm, of course. So, our worm has eyes.

Things to Do

- Grow grass in a plastic cup.
- Take a discovery trip to a patch of grass to find insects, flowers, and weeds. Mark each in a pad with a drawing.
- Make balloon worms from very long balloons and decorate them with felt-tip markers.
- Create **a worm farm.**
  1. Fill a fish bowl with layers of soil and dead leaves. Sprinkle water on each layer.
  2. Add worms.
  3. Wrap the bowl in dark paper to encourage the worms to live close to the glass. Unwrap the bowl to view the worms.
  4. *For care:* Feed the worms dead leaves, grass, or lettuce; keep the soil moist (never wet).

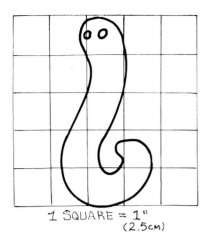

1 SQUARE = 1"
(2.5 CM)

Instructions

LETTER PAGE

1. **Patterns**—Draw a free-form worm on a 2½ × 5-inch (6.25 × 12.5-cm) piece of paper, or enlarge the worm on the grid (1 square = 1 inch or 2.5 cm). (See "Grids," p. 8.) The sun is a 3-inch (7.5-cm) circle. Trace *Gg*.

2. Using the patterns, cut appliqués from felt. Also cut 1 × 7-inch (2.5 × 17.5-cm) strips in different shades of green for the blades of grass.

3. Pin appliqués, except the strips, on the page, the sun below *Gg*, the worm 1¼ inches (3.12 cm) up from the bottom edge. Sew them in place.

4. Pin the strips side by side on the page, a little up from the bottom edge. Sew them in place across the bottom sides.

5. Cut points into the strips to create blades of grass in varying heights. The worm should be covered and the sun half exposed.

6. Print the words "GRASS" and "Behind" with fabric paints. Draw decorative details. The dragonfly is a commercial appliqué; create your own if you wish.

LETTER TOY

1. Draw a large *G* on paper for the pattern.

2. Using the pattern, cut out two felt letters.

3. Cut narrow blades of grass, as tall as the letter, to fit across the left side. Also cut out a small worm and a sun.

4. Sew the worm on the left side of a letter, the sun on the right. Sew the grass over the worm, along the bottom edges.

5. Sew the letters together with a little stuffing between them.

6. Draw decorative details with fabric paints.

GRASS

Behind

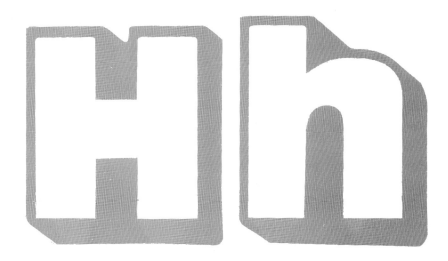

HELICOPTER

Spin

Spin the blades of the helicopter.

Discuss

- Things that *spin*—windmill, fan, pin-wheel, boat propeller, hands of a clock
- What makes things spin—wind, water (waterwheel), motor, windup spring (toy)
- Rotation and revolution—earth, moon, sun
- Differences between a helicopter and an airplane

Things to Do

- Play with pinwheels.
- Spin in place holding a crêpe paper streamer.
- Here's a **spin the bottle** game.
  1. Cut out a circle, using an entire sheet of poster board.
  2. Divide the circle into eight wedges.
  3. Write an activity in each wedge—like "dance a silly dance."
  4. Spin a plastic bottle in the middle of the circle. The neck points to the activity.

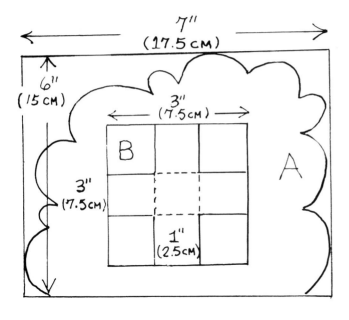

6. Print the words "HELICOPTER" and "Spin" with fabric paints. Draw decorative details.

LETTER TOY

1. Draw a large *H* on paper for the pattern.
2. Using the pattern, cut out two felt letters.
3. Sew the two letters together with a little stuffing between them.
4. Make two propellers and attach them to the top of the letter as described above.

Instructions

LETTER PAGE

1. **Patterns**—Draw a free-form cloud (A) and a propeller (B) to the dimensions shown. The helicopter is a squat 4 × 6-inch (10 × 15-cm) oval. Trace *Hh*.
2. Using the patterns, cut the appliqués from felt. Cut out two propellers. Also cut out a window, two wheels, and a 2½-inch (6.25-cm) strip for the propeller shaft.
3. Sew the window and the right wheel on the helicopter.
4. Pin the appliqués (except the propeller) on the page, with the helicopter overlapping the cloud. Tuck the other wheel and the shaft under the helicopter. Sew everything in place.
5. To construct the propeller, sew the two shapes together and attach them to the top of the shaft. (See "Moveable Appliqués," "Free Movement Appliqués," p. 10.)

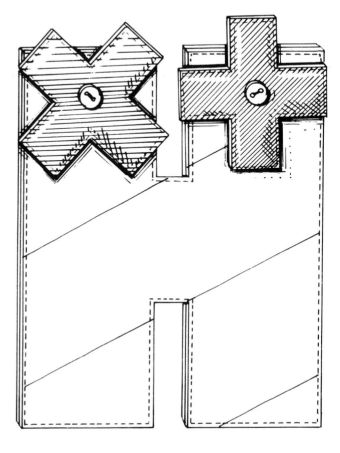

HELICOPTER

Spin

ICE CREAM

Stack

ICE CREAM CONE

Stack

Stack the scoops of ice cream, from large to small, on the cone.

Discuss

- Things that are *stacked*—cans and boxes, books, acrobats, sheets of paper, sandwich fixings
- Four basic food groups—poultry, meat, and legumes; dairy; fruits and vegetables; bread and cereals
- Flavors and favorites
- Different ice cream treats—ice cream cake, ice cream sandwich, ice cream soda, sundae, float

Things to Do

- Make ice cream sandwiches with cookies and ice cream.
- Invent silly flavors—onion chip, corn flakes and bananas, maple chestnut, or no-flavor ice cream
- Create an **ice cream clown.**
  1. Scoop ice cream on a plate.
  2. Press a candy or dried fruit face into the ice cream.
  3. Top with an ice cream cone hat.
  4. Spoon a whipped cream collar around the scoop.

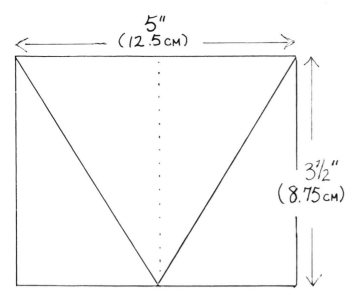

5"
(12.5 cm)

3½"
(8.75 cm)

LETTER TOY

1. Draw the tall letter *I* on paper for the pattern. Divide it into three equal parts.
2. Using one part, cut out six scoop shapes, each two in an ice cream color.
3. Sew each two squares together, with self-fastening tape sewn to appropriate places.
4. Stack the shapes to create the letter *I*.

Instructions

LETTER PAGE

1. **Patterns**—Draw an ice cream cone to the dimensions shown. Draw three ice cream scoops in diminishing sizes. Trace *Ii*.
2. Using the patterns, cut out felt appliqués. Cut out two shapes for each scoop. Also cut out a cherry and designs for the cone.
3. Sew the designs to the cone.
4. Pin the cone and the letters on the page and sew them in place.
5. To construct each scoop (see "Independent Appliqués," p. 10), sew self-fastening tape near the top of one shape and in the middle of the other, before sewing both together. You can sew on felt highlights, if you wish, before assembling.
6. Print the words "ICE CREAM" and "Stack" with fabric paints.
7. Add sequin confetti, if you wish.

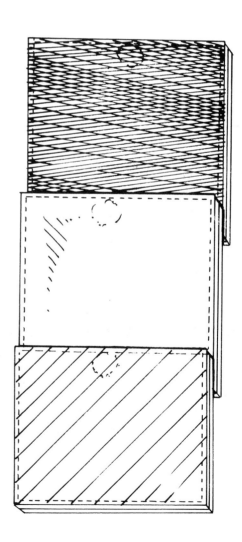

JELLYBEANS

Full, Empty

Fill and empty the candy machine with jellybeans.

Discuss

- Things that can be *filled* and *emptied*—drinking glass, suitcase, dish, wastebasket, Christmas stocking
- Jellybeans and the Easter bunny
- Favorite colors and flavors of jellybeans
- Favorite sweet treats

Things to Do

- Brush teeth after eating jellybeans and other sweets.
- Decorate a cake with jellybeans.
- Guess how many jellybeans (from six to ten) are in a small jar or glass.
- Create a **jellybean tree.**
  1. Mix plaster of Paris or other cement in a coffee can, one-third full.
  2. Insert a twig into the plaster.
  3. Tie small bundles of plastic-wrapped jellybeans to the branch after the plaster hardens. Keep play scissors in the can for cutting off the bundles.

Instructions

LETTER PAGE

1. **Patterns**—Make the globe a 6-inch (15-cm) circle with a slice removed to form a straight edge. Make the base from a rectangle 3 × 4½ inches (7.5 × 11.25 cm). Trace *Jj*.
2. Using the patterns, cut out felt appliqués. Also cut out two rectangles for the base and many colorful jellybeans.
3. Sew the rectangles together, one on top of the other.
4. Pin the appliqués to the page.
5. Cut a piece of clear plastic to fit on the lower two-thirds of the globe. Use heavy freezer bags or plastic sold by the yard.
6. Sew the appliqués in place.
7. Print the words "JELLYBEANS," "Full," and "Empty" with fabric paints. Draw highlights on the jellybeans.

LETTER TOY

1. Draw a large *J* on paper for the pattern.
2. Using the pattern, cut out two felt letters. Also cut out many colorful jellybeans.
3. Sew self-fastening tape scattered on one letter and to the jellybeans.
4. Sew the letters together with a little stuffing between them.

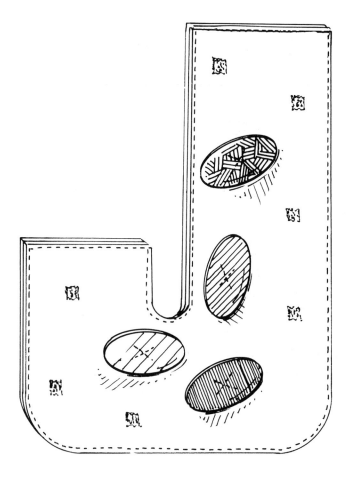

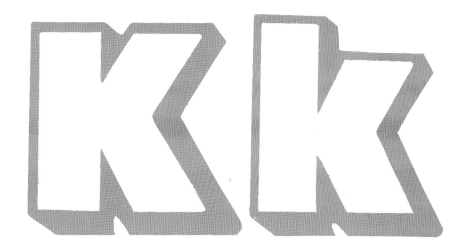

KANGAROO

Zipper

Put the baby kangaroo into its mother's pocket and zip up the pocket.

Discuss

- Things that have *pockets* and *zippers*—shirt, jacket, handbag, snowsuit, jeans, knapsack
- *Marsupials,* animals that carry their young in pouches—koala, opossum, Tasmanian wolf, wombat
- Australia's unique platypus
- Other animals that hop—rabbit, hare, squirrel, bird, frog

Things to Do

- Play hopscotch.
- Zipping and unzipping zippers; putting things into pockets and taking them out.
- Create **zip-apart pictures.**
  1. Glue a piece of paper to each side of a zipper. Do not cover the teeth.
  2. Filling in both sides of the paper, draw an object to be cut in half, like an apple or a twin ice pop.
  3. Unzip the zipper to cut the drawing in half. Zip up.

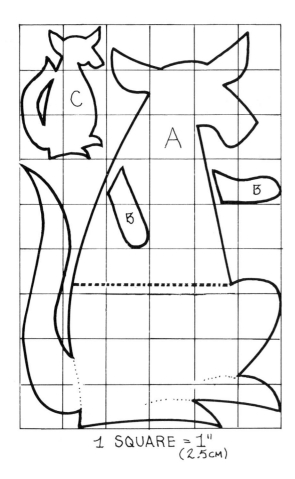

1 SQUARE = 1"
(2.5 CM)

Instructions

LETTER PAGE

1. **Patterns**—Enlarge the mother (A) and baby (C), and the arms (B) placed on the grid (1 square = 1 inch or 2.5 cm). (See "Grids," p. 8.) Trace *Kk*.
2. Using the patterns, cut out felt appliqués. Cut out two baby kangaroos.
3. Cut the mother kangaroo in two, using the heavy dotted line on the grid as a guide.
4. Sew the two halves to a zipper, with the excess extending out on one end.
5. Pin the appliqués (except the kangaroo baby) on the page.

6. Sew the appliqués in place, adding extra stitching when crossing the zipper. Cut away the excess zipper.
7. Print the words "KANGAROO" and "Zipper" with fabric paints. Draw decorative details.
8. Sew the baby kangaroo shapes together.

LETTER TOY

1. Draw a large *K* on paper for the pattern.
2. Using the pattern, cut out two felt letters.
3. Sew the letters together.
4. Cut out several narrow channels through both letters for the zippers.
5. Tuck zippers in the channels, after adding a little stuffing between the letters. Sew them in place.

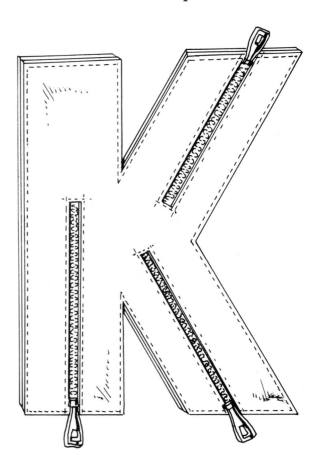

K k KANGAROO

Zipper

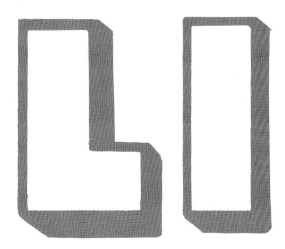

LOLLIPOP

Shapes

Match the lollipop shapes to their corresponding shapes on the page.

Discuss

- Things that have square, circular, oval, and rectangular *shapes*—toy block, sun, ladybug, cereal box
- Other shapes—triangle, diamond, star, heart, teardrop, hexagon, octagon
- Other tasty foods on sticks—corn dog, shish kebab, ice pop
- Favorite lollipop colors and flavors

Things to Do

- Brush teeth after eating lollipops and other sweets.
- Take a discovery trip around the house, neighborhood, countryside, or beach to find things shaped like squares, circles, ovals, or rectangles.
- Make **lollipop cookies.**
  1. Add frosting between two round cookies with an ice cream stick between them.
  2. Bake rounded drops of cookie dough with ice cream sticks inserted.

Instructions

LETTER PAGE

1. **Patterns**—The circle, square, oval, and rectangle do not exceed 2¼ inches (5.6 cm) in width. Trace *Ll*.
2. Using the patterns, cut out appliqués from felt. Cut two for each lollipop. Also cut smaller, similar lollipop shapes from gray or a neutral color of felt. Cut out sticks and highlights.
3. To construct the lollipops (see "Independent Appliqués," p. 10), sew each two shapes together. One side has a highlight sewn or glued in place, the other side has self-fastening tape.
4. Sew self-fastening tape to the middle of each gray shape.
5. Arrange the sticks, gray shapes, and letters on the page. Sew them in place.
6. Print the words "LOLLIPOP" and "Shapes" with fabric paints.

LETTER TOY

1. Draw a large *L* on paper for the pattern.
2. Using the pattern, cut out two felt letters.
3. Construct a square, circle, oval, and rectangle (as described in the letter page) to fit on the letter.
4. Sew self-fastening tape to a letter.
5. Sew the letters together with a little stuffing between them.

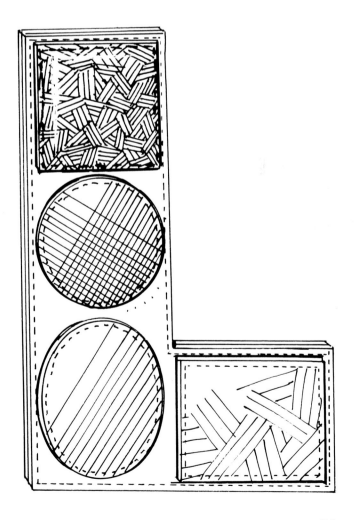

Ll

LOLLIPOP

Shapes

Mm

MAILBOX

Textures

MAILBOX

Textures

Raise the flag when textured letters are in the mailbox, and lower the flag when you remove them.

Discuss

- Things with different *textures*—rug, wool mitten, sandpaper, cotton ball, cat fur
- The post office and how mail goes from one place to another
- Pony Express
- Occasions for greeting cards—holidays, birthdays, sickness

Things to Do

- Start a postcard collection in a photo album.
- Start a stamp collection.
- Take a trip to the post office to mail a letter and buy stamps.
- Decorate inexpensive envelopes using crayons, markers, stickers, and rubber stamps.
- Create a **feely box.**
  1. Cut away a circle from the short side of a shoe, saltine, or graham cracker box that's large enough for a child's hand to pass through.
  2. Collect small items with different textures and put them in the box.
  3. Have the child try to identify the textures and items.

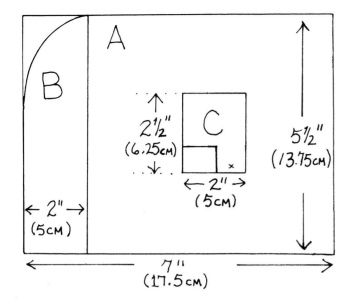

A

↑
2½"
(6.25cm)
↓

C

← 2" →
(5cm)

5½"
(13.75cm)

B

← 2" →
(5cm)

← 7" →
(17.5cm)

Instructions

LETTER PAGE

1. **Patterns**—Draw the mailbox (A), the door (B), and the flag (C) to the dimensions given. Trace *Mm*.
2. Using the patterns, cut appliqués from felt. Cut out two flags.
3. Pin the remaining appliqués on the page. Do not sew the mailbox along the left edge. Sew the door only along the bottom edge.
4. To construct the flag, sew the two shapes together. Attach the flag to the top of the mailbox at the right corner (see "Moveable Appliqués," "Free Movement," p. 10).
5. Cut small envelopes from materials with different textures—fake fur, velvet, burlap, oil cloth, plastic, or what you can find. Sew a fabric stamp on each.
6. Print "MAILBOX" and "Textures" with fabric paints.

LETTER TOY

1. Draw a large *M* on paper for the pattern.
2. Using the pattern, cut out two felt letters.
3. Sew on semicircles of different textured fabrics to one letter as shown.

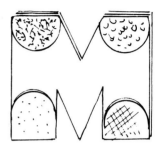

4. Sew the letters together with the textures inside. Leave the top and bottom sides of the letters unsewn.
5. Insert a finger to discover the hidden textures.

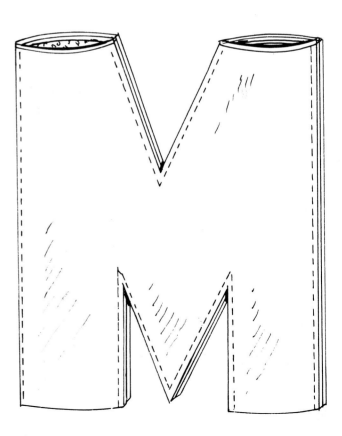

NEST

Big, Small

Place the big owls high in the nest and the small owls under them.

Discuss

- Things that are *big*—elephant, whale, house, mountain, dinosaur; things that are *small*—peas, chocolate chips, ant, mouse, chipmunk
- Biggest and smallest birds—ostrich and hummingbird
- Animals, besides birds, that build nests—rabbit, squirrel, mouse, fish

Things to Do

- Read Edward Lear's poem "The Owl and the Pussycat."
- Collect examples of small and large rocks, flowers, buttons, acorns, seashells, and more.
- Using a guidebook on birds, begin bird-watching. Record each sighting with a drawing.
- Make a **quill pen.**
  1. Find a large feather in the woods.
  2. Cut the end of the quill into a point.
  3. Cut a short slit from the tip into the point.
  4. Use food colors or weak water colors to print letters and draw fun shapes.

Nn NEST

Big•Small

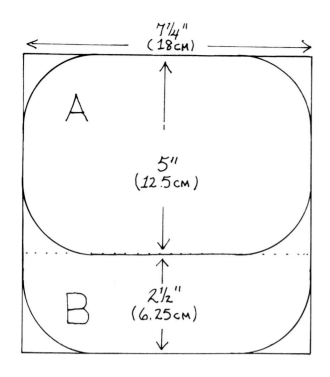

7¼"
(18cm)

A

5"
(12.5cm)

B

2½"
(6.25cm)

6. Print the words "NEST," "Big," and "Small" with fabric paints. Draw decorative details.

LETTER TOY

1. Draw a large *N* on paper for the pattern.
2. Using the pattern, cut out two felt letters.
3. Make three owls as described above in the letter page.
4. Sew self-fastening tape to one letter where the owls roost. Sew on leaves.
5. Sew the letters together with a little stuffing between them.

Instructions

LETTER PAGE

1. **Patterns**—Draw the upper nest (A) and lower nest (B) to the dimensions shown. Make the big owls 2½-inch (6.25-cm) circles and the small owls 1¾-inch (4.37 cm) circles. Trace *Nn*.
2. Using the patterns, cut appliqués from felt. Cut two circles for each owl. Also cut out the eyes, beaks, feet, and leaves.
3. Sew a crisscross design on the lower nest. Sew self-fastening tape on the upper nest where the birds sit.
4. Pin the appliqués on the page and sew them in place.
5. To construct the owls (see "Independent Appliqués," p. 10), sew or glue the birds' features to one of each pair of circles, and self-fastening tape to the other. Sew matching circles together.

OYSTER

Lift Up

Lift up the oyster shell to see the oyster and the pearl inside.

Discuss

- Hinged things that you can *lift up*—jewelry box lid, cover of a book, piano key cover, bakery box lid
- Other creatures that live in shells—clam, mollusk, mussel, snail, turtle, hermit crab
- How an oyster makes a pearl
- Things made with pearls—ring, necklace, bracelet, earrings, tie pin

Things to Do

- Make sand castles using shells for decorations.
- Collect shells in jars.
- Read the poem "The Walrus and the Carpenter" in Lewis Carroll's *Through the Looking-Glass*.
- Make a **jumbo oyster.**
  1. Cut two lightweight paper plates into identical oystershells.
  2. Staple the shells together at the narrow ends.
  3. Draw an oyster and a pearl on the inside shell.

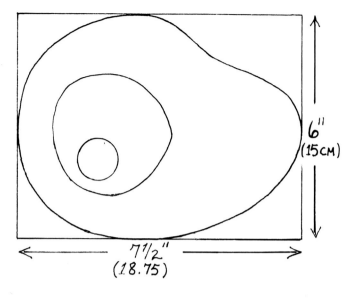

6"
(15CM)

7¹/₂"
(18.75)

LETTER TOY

1. Draw a large *O* on paper for the pattern.
2. Using the pattern, cut out two felt letters. From a different color of felt, cut out two flaps slightly larger than the letter's middle opening.
3. Sew a pearl with a face to one flap.
4. Lay the flap with the pearl over the opening of one letter, and sew it in place.
5. Sew the letters together with a little stuffing between them.
6. Sew the remaining flap to the letter, along the top edge.

Instructions

LETTER PAGE

1. Draw a free-form oystershell to the dimensions given. Draw an oyster and a pearl. Trace *Oo*.
2. Using the patterns, cut out appliqués from felt. Cut out two oystershells, one slightly shorter than the other on the wide end.
3. Sew the pearl to the oyster, and sew the oyster to the larger shell.
4. Pin the appliqués, except the top shell, on the page and sew them in place.
5. Create a shell design on the top shell with stitching or fabric paint.
6. Sew the top shell to the bottom shell along the curve of the narrow end.
7. Print the words "OYSTER" and "Lift Up" with fabric paints. Draw bubbles. The fish are commercial appliqués; add some if you wish.

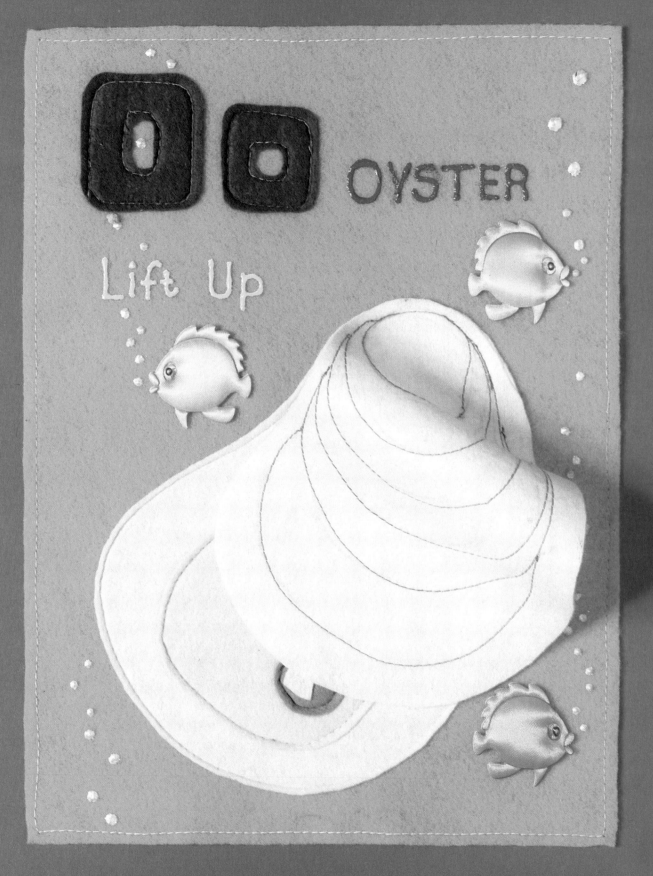

O o OYSTER

Lift Up

PANDA

Button

Button the panda's black eye patches onto the button eyes.

Discuss

- Things that have *buttons*—blouse, shirt, jacket, pants, vest
- Whether a panda is a bear
- Where pandas live and what kind of leaves they eat
- Raccoons—panda's cousins

Things to Do

- Practise buttoning and unbuttoning clothing.
- Start a unique button collection.
- Make button pictures by gluing small, flat buttons on a coloring book drawing.
- Create **panda pancakes.**
  1. Add powdered cocoa to a small amount of pancake batter until it turns dark brown.
  2. Spoon regular batter into large, round pancakes.
  3. Quickly spoon a little brown batter onto the pancake for the bear's ears, eye patches, and nose.
  4. Add raisin eyes.

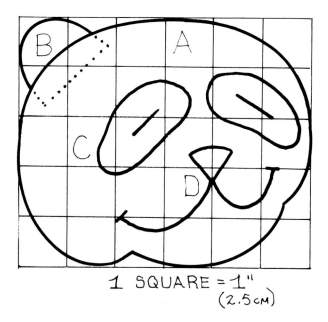

1 SQUARE = 1"
(2.5 CM)

Instructions

LETTER PAGE

1. **Patterns**—Enlarge the panda's head
   (A), ears (B), eye patches (C), and
   nose (D) placed on the grid (1 square
   = 1 inch or 2.5 cm). (See "Grids,"
   p. 8.) Trace *Pp*.
2. Using the patterns, cut out appliqués
   from felt. Cut out two ears and two
   shapes for each eye patch. Also cut
   out leaves and a bow tie.
3. To construct the eye patches (see "Independent Appliqués," p. 10), sew
   each two together. Make buttonholes
   by hand or machine close to one end.
4. Pin the remaining appliqués on the
   page with the ears tucked under the
   head. Sew them in place.
5. Place the eye patches on the head
   and mark where you want to sew
   button eyes. Sew the buttons in
   place.
6. Print "PANDA" and "Button" with
   fabric paints.

7. Make the mouth from yarn, fabric
   paint, or embroidery.

LETTER TOY

1. Draw a large *P* on paper for the
   pattern.
2. Using the pattern, cut out two felt
   letters.
3. Sew a bow and add a smile to one
   letter.
4. Make eye patches and sew on buttons described in the letter page.
5. With ears tucked in at the top, sew
   the letters together with a little stuffing between them.

QUILT

Lace

65

QUILT

Lace

Lace the two halves of the quilt together.

Discuss

- Things you can *lace*—shoes, sneakers, clothing, football
- Different kinds of blankets—comforter, down quilt, electric blanket, baby blanket, beach blanket, Christmas tree blanket, throw
- Patchwork quilt (pioneer blanket)

Things to Do

- Practise lacing shoes and sneakers.
- Color worn-out shoe laces with permanent markers.
- Make a tiny quilt for a dollhouse bed.
- Create a **fabric collage.**
  1. Cut shapes in both prints and solid colors from fabric scraps.
  2. Paste the shapes on paper.

Instructions

LETTER PAGE

1. **Patterns**—Make the quilt's square 3¾ inches (9.5 cm). Trace *Qq*.
2. Using the pattern, cut out four different colored squares from felt.
3. Make three holes equally spaced along one side of each square. You can make holes with a paper punch or add grommets.
4. With the holes lined up, sew each two squares together with ⅛-inch (.3-cm) seams.
5. Pin the two sets of assembled squares on a page, with the holes on the inside. Sew each in place along the outer edge.
6. Feed a shoelace in and out of the holes.
7. Print "QUILT" and "Lace" with fabric paints.

LETTER TOY

1. Draw a large *Q* on paper and cut it into sections for the patterns.
2. Using the patterns, cut one of each section from a different color of felt, adding ¼ inch (.62 cm) extra on the cut lines for seam allowance.
3. Sew the sections together to form the letter. Press flat.
4. Cut a second letter using the reassembled letter as a pattern.
5. Sew the letters together with a little stuffing between them.
6. Punch holes or add grommets along opposite sides of the middle opening. Feed a shoelace in and out of the holes.

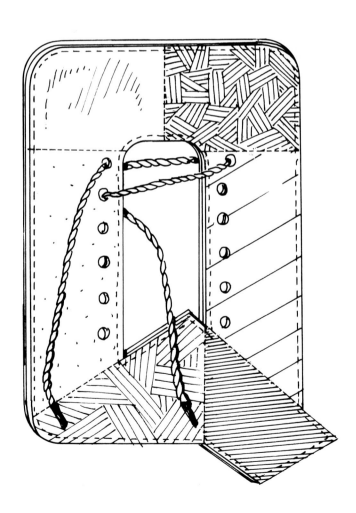

R r ROCKING HORSE

Back and Forth

ROCKING HORSE

Back and Forth

Move the rocking horse back and forth.

Discuss

- Things that rock *back and forth*—swing, rocking chair, clock pendulum, cradle, boat
- Other fabulous horses—unicorn, Pegasus (flying horse), horse of a different color from *The Wizard of Oz*
- Other favorite toys
- Rocking horse cousin—merry-go-round horse

Things to Do

- Rock a baby to sleep.
- Discover the Rocking-horse-fly in Lewis Carroll's *Through the Looking-Glass.*
- Recite the nursery rhyme "Rock-a-bye, Baby."
- Recite the nursery rhyme "Ride a Cock Horse to Banbury Cross."
- Make **rocking pictures.**
  1. Fold a piece of poster board in half.
  2. Draw a semicircle with the straight edge on the fold.
  3. Cut out with an even line, keeping a section of the fold uncut.
  4. Draw a picture on the front of the semicircle.
  5. Open the paper slightly and rock it on a flat surface.

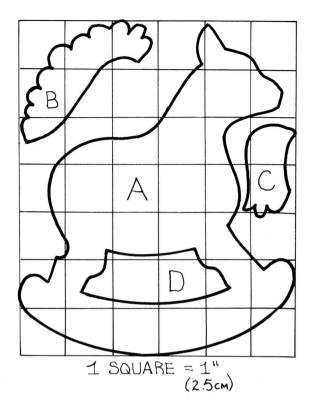

1 SQUARE = 1"
(2.5cm)

Instructions

LETTER PAGE

1. **Patterns**—Enlarge the rocking horse (A), mane (B), tail (C), and the open-space design (D) on the grid (1 square = 1 inch or 2.5 cm). (See "Grids," p. 8.) Trace *Rr*.
2. Using the patterns, cut appliqués from felt. Cut out two rocking horses.
3. Pin the letters on the page and sew them in place. Sew on rickrack for the ground.
4. To construct the horse, sew the open-space design on one rocking horse. Pin the mane and tail tucked between the horse shapes, and sew them together. Decorate with fabric paint and felt designs. Add a satin bow.

5. To attach the horse to the page, see "Moveable Appliqués," "Limited Movement," pp. 9–10.
6. Print the words "ROCKING HORSE" and "Back and Forth" with fabric paints. Draw decorative details.

LETTER TOY

1. Draw a large *R* in two sections on paper for the patterns. Both sections should overlap each other 1 inch (2.5 cm).
2. Using the patterns, cut out two shapes for each section.
3. Sew matching shapes together with a little stuffing between them.
4. Attach the two sections together as described in "Moveable Appliqués," "Limited Movement," pp. 9–10.

SNEAKERS

Left, Right

Unfasten and fasten the left and right sneakers.

Discuss

- Things that have a *left* and a *right* side—jacket, pants, cowboy boots, gloves
- Special foot coverings—bedroom slippers, ballerina shoes, rubber boots, golf shoes, sandals, hip boots for fishing
- Feet—toes, toenails, bones, heel, arch

Things to Do

- Trace feet on paper and color on fun designs.
- Recite the nursery rhyme "There Was an Old Woman Who Lived in a Shoe."
- Read Eugene Field's poem "Wynken, Blynken, and Nod," three fishermen who "sailed off in a wooden shoe."
- Create **crazy dances.**
  1. Draw left and right shoes many times on paper and cut them out.
  2. Create a dance pattern by laying the shoes on the floor in a repetitive left/right pattern.
  3. Following the shoes, step in rhythm to fast and slow music.

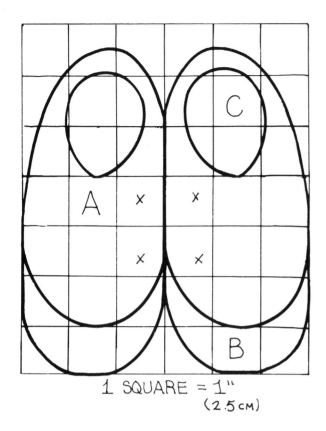

1 SQUARE = 1"
(2.5 CM)

Instructions

LETTER PAGE

1. **Patterns**—Enlarge the sneakers (A),
   the soles (B), and foot openings (C)
   on the grid (1 square = 1 inch or
   2.5 cm). (See "Grids," p. 8.) Also
   draw a tab 1 × 2½ inches (2.5 × 6.25
   cm), with one short end rounded.
   Trace Ss.
2. Using the patterns, cut out felt appliqués. Cut eight tabs.
3. Pin the appliqués (except the tabs)
   on the page and sew them in place.
4. Sew each two tabs together.
5. Sew two tabs on each sneaker, along
   the short sides.
6. Print the words "SNEAKERS,"
   "Left," and "Right" with fabric
   paints.

LETTER TOY

1. Draw a large *S* on paper for the
   pattern.
2. Using the pattern, cut out two felt
   letters. Also cut out two tabs, with
   one end rounded, and an *L* and an *R*.
3. Sew the *R* to the top end of one letter
   and the *L* to the bottom end.
4. Sew the letters together with a little
   stuffing between them.
5. Sew the tabs to the letter at the ends.

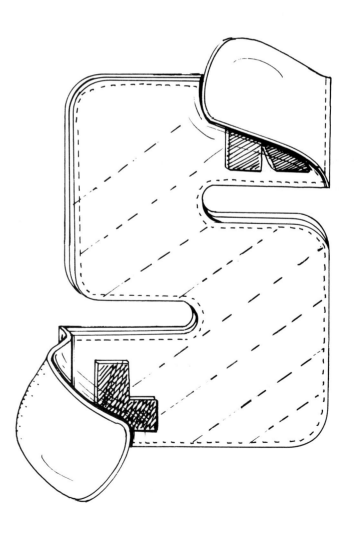

S s SNEAKERS

Left • Right

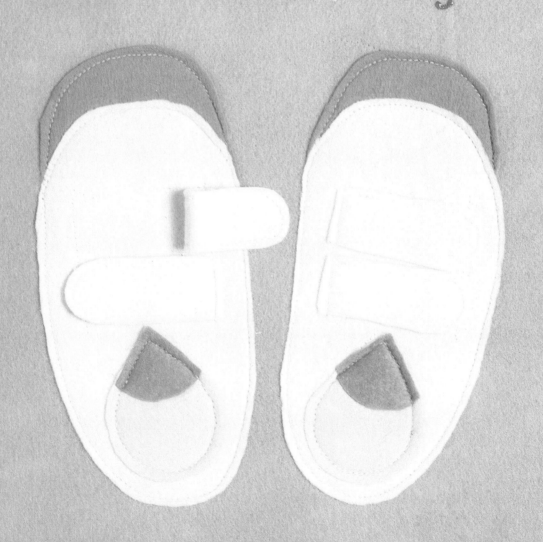

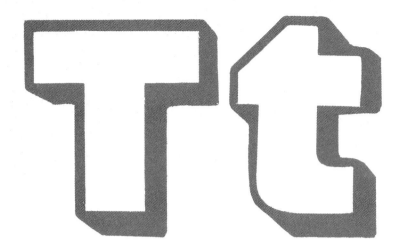

TREE

Day, Night

Change day to night by lifting up the day sky behind the tree.

Discuss

- Things visible in the sky during the *day*—sun, clouds, airplanes, birds, rainbow; *night*—moon, stars, planets, comets, Milky Way, fireflies
- Nocturnal animals—bat, raccoon, owl, mouse
- *Daytime activities*—breakfast, lunch, school, mow the lawn; *nighttime activities*—supper, bedtime story, sleep, dream
- Different kinds of trees

Things to Do

- Read Hans Christian Andersen's "The Story of What the Moon Saw."
- Look at the stars through binoculars or a telescope.
- Visit a planetarium.
- Check out a library book on stars, and look for constellations in the night sky.
- Make moon cookies by frosting large homemade or store-bought cookies, half with vanilla icing and half with chocolate icing.
- Make **leaf prints.**
  1. Place a leaf on paper, vein side up.
  2. Lay lightweight paper on the leaf.
  3. With the flat side of a crayon, rub the paper to bring out the impression of the leaf.

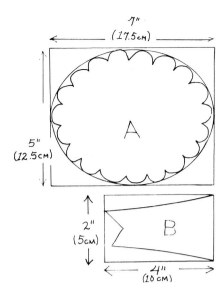

Instructions

LETTER PAGE

1. **Patterns**—Draw the foliage (A) and the trunk (B) to the dimensions shown. Trace *Tt*.
2. Using the patterns, cut out appliqués from felt. Cut two trunks. Also cut out clouds, the sun, a butterfly, stars, and the moon.
3. The day sky is light blue; the night sky is a dark blue or purple. The day sky is 1 inch (2.5 cm) shorter than the night sky at the bottom.
4. Pin the appliqués to their appropriate skies and sew them in place.
5. To construct the tree, sew the trunks together with the foliage between them.
6. Sew the tree to the center bottom of the night sky with two parallel lines of stitches.
7. Lay the day sky on the night sky, with top edges flush, and sew them together at the top.

8. Print the words "TREE," "Day," and "Night" with fabric paints. Draw decorative details.

LETTER TOY

1. Draw a large *T* on paper for the pattern.
2. Using the pattern, cut two letters from light blue felt and two from dark blue.
3. Cut free-form appliqués for day and night.
4. Sew appropriate appliqués to one of each two letters.
5. Sew each two matching-color letters together, with a little stuffing between them.
6. Punch or cut two holes into the top of both constructed letters, with the holes lining up.
7. Tie the letter together with loops of yarn.

T t TREE

Day

Night

Night

UMBRELLA

Fold Over

To open the umbrella for a rain shower, fold over the panel with the closed umbrella.

Discuss

- Things that *fold over*—blanket on a bed, omelette, sweater cuffs
- Special umbrellas—beach umbrella, paper party umbrella, rainy-day umbrella, patio umbrella
- Why rain is important
- The story of Noah's Ark
- How a parachute is a jumbo umbrella

Things to Do

- Help fold laundry.
- Make folded paper fans.
- Measure a rainfall by setting an open jar outside.
- Create **paint blots.**
  1. Fold a sheet of paper in half.
  2. Drop thick squiggles of poster paint on one half.
  3. Fold the paper over and rub hard in all directions.
  4. Open the paper to see the paint blot.

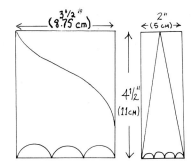

Instructions

LETTER PAGE

1. **Patterns**—Draw the umbrella shapes to the dimensions given. Trace *Uu*.
2. Using the patterns, cut out appliqués from felt. Cut out two open umbrella halves. Also cut out two handles and clumps of grass and a sun.
3. Pin an open umbrella on the page (its straight side on an imaginary center line), a handle, letters, and grass. Sew everything in place.
4. Cut a second page, the same color, in half.
5. Pin the closed umbrella, handle, and sun on one half. Pin the other open umbrella to the other half, with the straight side flush with the edge of the page. Both open umbrella halves should be aligned with each other. Sew them in place, adding extra stitch details.
6. Sew the half pages together.
7. Place the half page over the right side of the whole page, and sew in place along the left side of the half page.
8. Print "UMBRELLA" and "Fold Over" with fabric paints. Paint raindrops on the open umbrella page and other decorative details.

LETTER TOY

1. Draw a large *U* on paper for the pattern.
2. Using the pattern, cut out three felt letters.
3. Add a sun to the left side of a letter and a cloud and raindrops to the other side (A).
4. Sew the appliqué letter to another letter with a little stuffing between them.
5. Cut the remaining letter in half.
6. On one half (cut edge on the right), add a cloud and drops (B), and add sun rays on the reverse side (C). Sew the flap to the center of the stuffed letter.

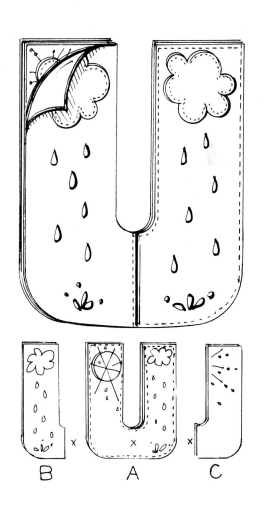

Uu

UMBRELLA

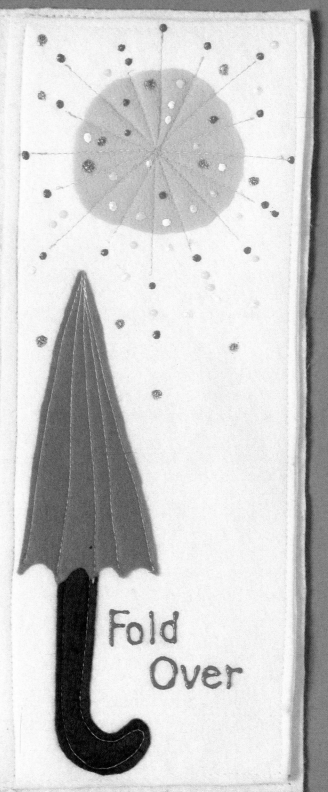

Fold
Over

VALENTINE

Pocket

Place the sweetheart in the pocket on the valentine.

Discuss

- Things that have *pockets*—shirt, shorts, pants, skirt, jacket, coat, apron
- Things put in pockets—hands, keys, handkerchief, wallet, money
- Discuss the legend of St. Valentine and the myth of Cupid
- Things that are also red—apples, fire truck, stop sign, traffic light, cherries

Things to Do

- Make heart-shaped cookies with red icing.
- Make Valentine's Day cards.
- Create a **paper heart garland.**
  1. Cut red construction paper in three along the length.
  2. Fold the strips, back and forth, into several sections.
  3. Draw a heart encompassing the top paper.
  4. Cut out the heart, leaving part of the folded edges uncut.
  5. Glue or tape many heart chains together to form a long garland.

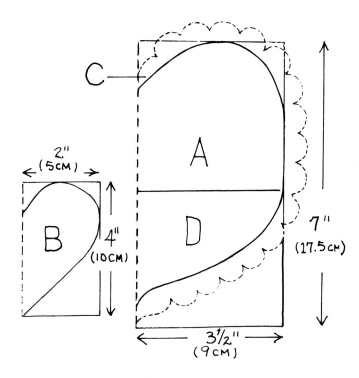

2" (5CM)

B

4" (10CM)

C

A

D

7" (17.5CM)

3½" (9CM)

Instructions

LETTER PAGE

1. **Patterns**—Draw the valentine (A) and the sweetheart (B) to the dimensions given. Using the valentine pattern, cut out lace with a scalloped edge (C), making it larger than the valentine. Also cut out a pattern for the pocket (D). Trace *Vv*.
2. Using the patterns, cut out appliqués from felt. Place the straight side of the valentine, sweetheart, and lace on the fold of the folded felt. Cut out two sweethearts. Also cut out arms, eyes, and a mouth.
3. To make the sweetheart (see "Independent Appliqués," p. 10), sew the eyes and mouth to one heart, before sewing both together with the hands tucked between them.
4. Pin the remaining appliqués on the page. Place the valentine on the lace

(punch holes with a paper punch) and the pocket on the valentine. Sew them in place.
5. Print the words "VALENTINE" and "Pocket" with fabric paints. Draw decorative details and add spangles.

LETTER TOY

1. Draw a large *V* on paper for the pattern.
2. Using the pattern, cut out two felt letters. Also cut out a pocket for the lower half of the letter.
3. With the pocket in place, sew the letters together with a little stuffing between them.
4. Construct the smaller sweetheart appliqué as described in the letter page.

VALENTINE

Pocket

WEATHER VANE

North

East

West

South

WEATHER VANE

North, South, East, West

Place North, South, East, and West in their proper places on the weather vane.

Discuss

- Things that are found *north*—Santa Claus, North Pole, polar bears; *east*—countries, rising sun; *west*—ocean, setting sun; *south*—Antarctica, penguins, South Pole
- How a weather vane works
- How to tell time with a sundial
- The North Star
- The direction of approaching weather after you watch the weather report

Things to Do

- Go for a walk with a compass.
- Find in an atlas what countries are north, south, east, and west of home.
- Look for moss and lichens on a tree to find north (in the Northern Hemisphere).
- Create a **weather vane.**
  1. On the top lid of a food can, print *N*, *S*, *E*, and *W* near the rim and equally spaced, with fabric paint or a permanent marker.
  2. Glue an empty thread spool on the middle of the lid.
  3. Cut a 3-inch (7.5-cm) arrow from cardboard, and tape it to an end of a drinking straw.
  4. Insert the straw into the spool's center hole. Place the weather vane in a breeze with *N* facing north.

Instructions

LETTER PAGE

1. **Patterns**—Draw *N*, *S*, *E*, and *W* 2¼ inches (5.62 cm) high on paper, or trace the letters from the book. Trace *Ww*.
2. Using the patterns, cut out appliqués from felt. Cut two of each directional letter. Also cut two 1 × 6½-inch (2.5 × 16.25-cm) strips.
3. Pin the strips, crossing one another, and *Ww* on the page. Sew them in place.
4. Sew self-fastening tape to the four ends of the cross.
5. To construct *N*, *S*, *E*, and *W* (see "Independent Appliqués," p. 10), sew self-fastening tape to one of each of the two letters, with the letter facing the wrong direction. Sew each pair of letters together.
6. Print the words "WEATHER VANE," "North," "South," "East," and "West" with fabric paints. Draw decorative details.

LETTER TOY

1. Draw a large *W* on paper for your pattern.
2. Using the pattern, cut out two felt letters. Also cut out *N*, *S*, *E*, and *W*.
3. With a letter tilted so that the top left end faces north, sew the *N*, *S*, *E*, and *W* in their appropriate positions.
4. Sew the letters together with a little stuffing between them.

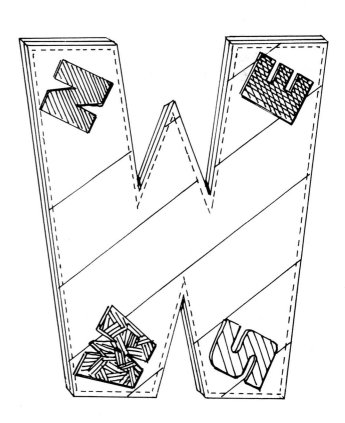

X x XYLOPHONE

Colors

XYLOPHONE

Colors

Arrange the xylophone bars by size to create the order of the colors of the rainbow.

Discuss

- Things that have many *colors*—rainbow, box of crayons, paint pallet, bag of jellybeans, gum-ball machine
- Favorite color or colors
- Other musical instruments that are struck—drum, gong, bell, marimba, rhythm sticks

Things to Do

- Go on a color safari.
- Sing "Somewhere over the Rainbow" and the "Rainbow Connection."
- Blow bubbles in the sunlight to see the colors of the rainbow.
- Recite the nursery rhyme "Little Boy Blue."
- Read the tale "Little Red Riding Hood."
- Read Gelett Burgess's poem "I Never Saw a Purple Cow."
- Make a **rainbow gelatin dessert.**
  1. Dissolve lime (green) gelatin according to directions.
  2. Fill clear plastic cups one-sixth full.
  3. When firm, add berry (blue) gelatin to the lime layer.
  4. Continue with grape (purple), strawberry (red), orange (orange), and lemon (yellow) gelatins.

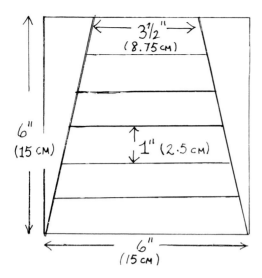

3½" (8.75 cm)

6" (15 cm)

1" (2.5 cm)

6" (15 cm)

Instructions

LETTER PAGE

1. **Patterns**—Draw the xylophone shape with six equal sections following the dimensions shown. Trace *Xx*.
2. Using the patterns, cut appliqués from felt. Cut a xylophone shape in a neutral color, before cutting the pattern into six bars along the division lines. Cut two of each bar in progressively larger sizes out of yellow, orange, red, purple, blue, and green—in that rainbow order.
3. To construct the xylophone bars (see "Independent Appliqués," p. 10), sew self-fastening tape to one shape of each color, before sewing matching shapes together.
4. Pin the remaining appliqués on the page and sew them in place.
5. Sew self-fastening tape equally spaced on the neutral-colored xylophone for each bar.
6. Print the words "XYLOPHONE" and "Colors" with fabric paints. Draw colored notes.

LETTER TOY

1. Draw two large crisscrossing bars on paper to form an *X*. One crossbar will serve as the pattern.
2. Using the pattern, cut out four crossbars from felt.
3. Sew yellow, orange, and red ribbons along the length of one crossbar. Sew purple, blue, and green ribbons on a second crossbar (facing the opposite direction). Trim away excess ribbon.
4. Sew the ribboned crossbars to the plain crossbars with a little stuffing between them.
5. To form an *X*, attach the two bars together at their centers with self-fastening tape. Unattach and lay side by side to form the rainbow.

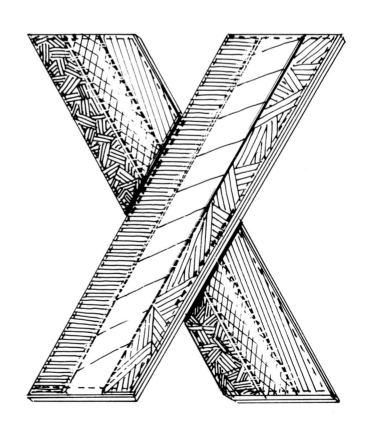

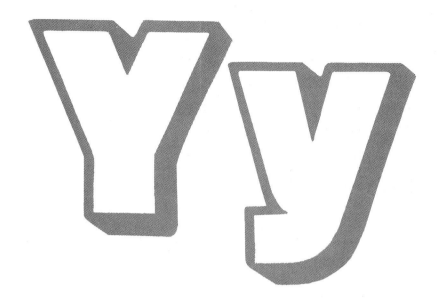

YO-YO

Up, Down

Pull the top string to make the yo-yo go up; pull the bottom string to make it go down.

Discuss

- Things that go *up* and *down*—elevator, escalator, zipper, airplane, window shade.
- What goes up but never goes down? Your age.
- Things that spin—Frisbee, globe of the earth, top, pinwheel, planets.

Things to Do

- Walk up and down stairs and count the stairs.
- Throw objects of different weights into the air, and compare how they return to the ground—ball/feather, rice/confetti, Frisbee/paper airplane.
- Play with a real yo-yo.
- Create a **parachute.**
  1. Tie 9 inches (22.5 cm) of string to each corner of a square paper napkin.
  2. Tie the ends of the string to a metal washer.
  3. Wrap the string around the washer and the napkin around the string, and toss it high into the air.

Instructions

LETTER PAGE

1. **Patterns**—The yo-yo is a 3-inch (7.5-cm) circle with a 2-inch (5-cm) inner circle. Trace *Yy*.
2. Using the patterns, cut out appliqués from felt. Cut out two yo-yos. Also cut two small narrow strips for attaching the yo-yo to the page.
3. Pin and sew *Yy* on the page.
4. Pin the strips centered on the page in line with each other and as far apart as possible. Sew them in place, leaving a channel in the middle for yarn to pass through.
5. Sew the inner circle to one yo-yo. Add a decorative spangle.
6. To construct the yo-yo (see "Independent Appliqués," p. 10), sew the two yo-yos together.
7. Punch two holes into the yo-yo, opposite each other near the edge. Tie yarn in each hole. You can also tuck string between the circles before sewing.

8. Feed the yarn through the strips, and tie the ends to rings or buttons or sew them on the felt. Trim away the excess.
9. Print the words "YO-YO," "Up," and "Down" with fabric paints. Draw decorative details.

LETTER TOY

1. Draw a large *Y* on paper for the pattern.
2. Using the pattern, cut out two letters. Also cut out two strips and two yo-yos.
3. Construct and attach the yo-yos to one letter as described for the letter page.
4. Sew the letters together with a little stuffing between them.

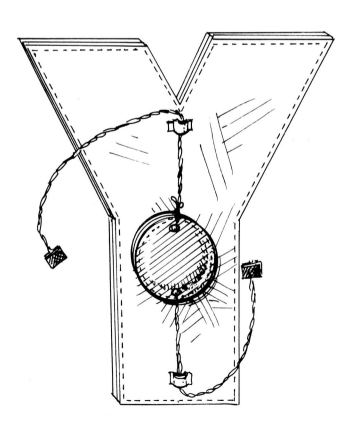

Y y

YO-YO

Up

Down

93

Zz

ZEBRA

Reverse

Reverse the zebra to change it from black with white stripes to white with black stripes.

Discuss

- Animals that are black and white—killer whale (Orca), zebra, skunk, white tiger; some birds, cats, and dogs (Dalmatian)
- Riddle of the zebra—white with black stripes or black with white stripes
- Other animals that live in Africa
- Noah's Ark

Things to Do

- Read Rudyard Kipling's *The Jungle Book.*
- Reverse your T-shirt.
- Hold a drawing in front of a mirror to see it reversed.
- Use the opposite hand (not your usual writing hand) to draw a picture.
- Reverse your steps to "Mother, May I?" commands.
- Visit a zoo.
- Make **silhouettes.**
  1. Cut a simple animal or any specific or undefined shape from black construction paper.
  2. Paste the cutout on white paper.

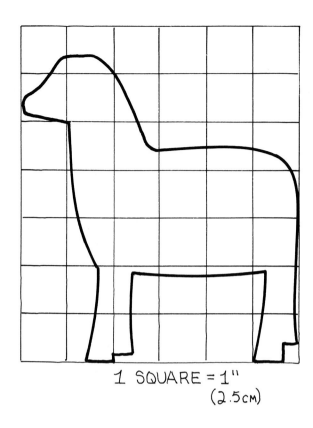

1 SQUARE = 1"
(2.5CM)

6. Print the words "ZEBRA" and "Reverse" with fabric paints.
7. Add a tree to the background with machine stitching, embroidery, or fabric paint.

LETTER TOY

1. Draw a large *Z* on paper for the pattern.
2. Using the pattern, cut out two felt letters, one black and one white. Also cut out black and white stripes.
3. Sew stripes on the letters.
4. Sew the letters together with a little stuffing between them.

Instructions

LETTER PAGE

1. **Patterns**—Enlarge the zebra on the grid (1 square = 1 inch or 2.5 cm). (See "Grids," p. 8.) Trace *Zz*.
2. Using the pattern, cut out appliqués from felt. Cut out one black zebra and one white. Also cut out black and white stripes, ears, and eyes.
3. Sew or glue stripes and eyes on the zebras. Sew self-fastening tape to the middle of each zebra.
4. To construct the zebra (see "Independent Appliqués," p. 10), sew the bodies together with the ears and small pieces of black and white yarn (mane and tail) tucked between them.
5. Pin the remaining appliqués on the page and sew them in place.

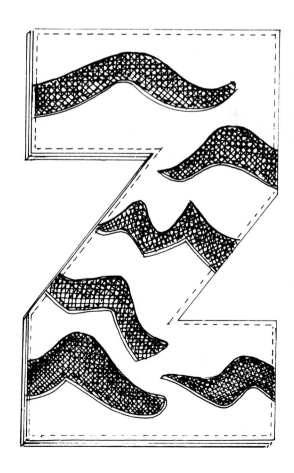

Zz

ZEBRA

Reverse

123 BOOK COVER

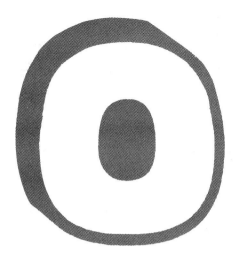

DOUGHNUT HOLE

Remove, Return

Remove and return the bite.

Discuss

- Things you can *remove* and *return*—book from a shelf, toys from a bin, hat from your head, cork from a bottle, clothes from a closet
- Favorite desserts
- Things that have holes—tire, ring, loose-leaf paper, saltshaker, drinking straw
- How doughnuts are made

Things to Do

- Add colorful sprinkles to desserts—pudding, gelatin, fruit cocktail, rice pudding.
- Draw doughnuts on paper using a compass. Color them in with fun frosting designs.
- Visit a bakery.
- Here's a **doughnut game.**
  1. Place doughnuts on plates.
  2. With the players' hands behind their backs, the first one to eat the doughnut without touching it with their hands wins.

123 Book Cover

1. **Patterns**—Draw a diamond, heart, and clover 4 inches (10 cm) high. Also draw or trace from the book the numbers *1*, *2*, and *3* to fit on the diamond, heart, and clover shapes.
2. Using the patterns, cut out the shapes in different colors. Cut out the numbers in constrasting colors.
3. Sew the numbers to the shapes.
4. Pin the shapes on the page, with each overlapping the other slightly. Sew them in place.
5. Sew on a decorative trim border.

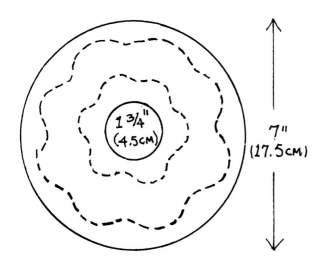

1 3/4"
(4.5cm)

7"
(17.5cm)

NUMBER TOY

1. Draw a large *0* on paper for the pattern.
2. Using the pattern, cut two felt zeros. Also cut out the icing.
3. Sew the icing to one of the zeros.
4. Place the zeros together and cut away a bite.
5. With a small piece of yarn tucked between each two matching shapes, sew them together with a little stuffing in between.
6. Cut out a bite from the doughnut, and sew it along the unfinished edges of both.
7. Tie the end of the yarn to a hole punched into the corner of the bite.

Instructions

NUMBER PAGE

1. **Patterns**—Make the doughnut according to the dimensions given. The icing is a wavy circle that fits on the doughnut. Trace the number *0* (zero).
2. Using the patterns, cut out the appliqués from felt.
3. Sew the icing on the doughnut.
4. Cut out a bite from the doughnut.
5. Pin the doughnut, without the bite, and the *0* on the page, and sew them in place.
6. Sew self-fastening tape to the back of the bite.
7. Sew self-fastening tape on the page where the bite will be placed.
8. Print the words "DOUGHNUT HOLE," "Remove," and "Return" with fabric paints. Paint decorative details.

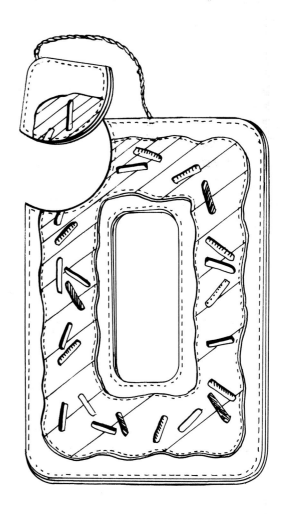

DOUGHNUT HOLE

Remove • Return

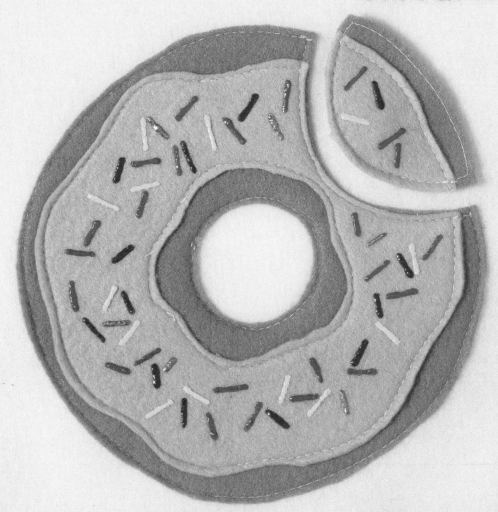

TULIP

Grow

TULIP

Grow

Push the stem up to make the flower grow.

Discuss

- Things that *grow*—people, flowers, trees, coral, fish, insects
- Where flowers grow—on sand dunes, along highways, in flower pots, in backyards, in the country
- Parts of the flower—stamen, petals, leaves, pistils, stem(s), roots
- Why bees are flowers' best friends

Things to Do

- Grow flower seeds in a pot.
- Help in a garden.
- Dry wild flowers and clover in a book.
- Recite the nursery rhyme "Mary, Mary Quite Contrary, How Does Your Garden Grow?"
- Make a **growth chart.**
  1. Cut sheets of green construction paper in half along the length.
  2. Glue the halves together to form a long flower stem (5 feet or 150 cm).
  3. Glue a large paper flower and leaves to the top of the stem.
  4. Starting at the bottom of the stem, mark inches (short lines) and feet (longer lines) or simply centimetres along with their number designations.
  5. Hang on a wall with the stem touching the floor. Add stickers to show new heights.

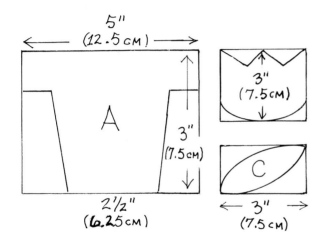

Instructions

NUMBER PAGE

1. **Patterns**—Cut the flowerpot (A), tulip (B), and leaf (C) to the dimensions given. Trace number *1*.
2. Using the patterns, cut out felt appliqués. Cut two flowers. Also cut out two 1×7-inch (2.5×17.5-cm) stems and two ½×3-inch (1.25×7.5-cm) tabs.
3. Sew the number and pot on the page. When sewing the pot, slightly buckle the middle and sew a 2-inch (5-cm) vertical channel.
4. To construct the tulip (see "Independent Appliqués," p. 10), sew the stems together. Then sew the flowers together with one stem end and the leaves tucked between them. For easier movement on the page, back the flower and stem with plastic wrap, cut to size.
5. Insert the stem through the pot's channel.
6. Sew the tabs to the end of the stem.
7. Print the words "TULIP" and "Grow" with fabric paints. Draw decorative details.

NUMBER TOY

1. Draw a large *1* on paper for the pattern.
2. Using the pattern, cut out two numbers. Also cut out two tulips, stems, leaves, and tabs.
3. Sew the numbers together with a little stuffing between them.
4. Cut two slits, 1 inch (2.5 cm) apart, through the assembled number. Hem both sides of each slit.
5. Construct the tulip, insert the stem through the slits, and add the tabs described above.

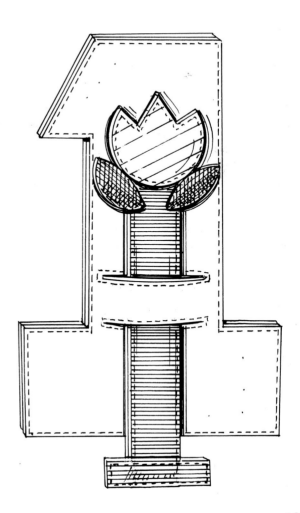

Z HANDS

Time

HANDS

Time

Move the hands to tell what time it is.

Discuss

- The *times of day*—dawn, morning, afternoon, dusk, evening, midnight
- Timekeepers—cuckoo clock, wristwatch, sundial, grandfather clock, water clock
- Things that come in twos—twins, mittens, shoes, eyes, ears, ice pops
- Other things that have numbers—typewriter, telephone, calculator, ruler, hopscotch

Things to Do

- Recite the nursery rhyme "Hickory, Dickory, Dock."
- Discover the White Rabbit who was late in Lewis Carroll's *Alice in Wonderland.*
- Show the time of day with outstretched arms.
- Create a **sundial.**
  1. Cut a 4-inch (10-cm) high triangle from paper.
  2. Slightly fold over one side and glue it to the middle of the underside of a paper plate.
  3. At noon, move the sundial so that the triangle's shadow is a thin line. Mark this point with a *12.*
  4. Study the movement of the shadow and guess the time.

Instructions

NUMBER PAGE

1. **Patterns**—The alarm clock is composed of circles—7-inch (17.5-cm) clock body, 5½-inch (13.75-cm) face, 2-inch (5-cm) bells with 1-inch (2.5-cm) caps, and 1¼-inch (3.125-cm) feet. Draw two hands, one shorter than the other, no longer than 3 inches (7.5 cm). Trace number *2*.
2. Using the patterns, cut appliqués from felt. Cut out two bells, caps, and feet, and two of each of the hands.
3. Sew the face to the clock.
4. Pin the appliqués (except the hands) on a page, with the bells and feet tucked under the clock. Sew them in place, adding the caps to the bells.
5. To construct the hands, sew each two together and attach them to the middle of the clock. (See "Free Movement Appliqués," p. 10.)
6. Print the words "HANDS" and "Time" and the numbers on the face with fabric paints. To make the alarm clock more authentic, draw a small alarmset dial on the clock's face.

NUMBER TOY

1. Draw a large *2* on paper for the pattern.
2. Using the pattern, cut out two felt numbers.
3. Sew the numbers together with a little stuffing between them.
4. Cut, assemble, and attach two hands as described in the letter page.

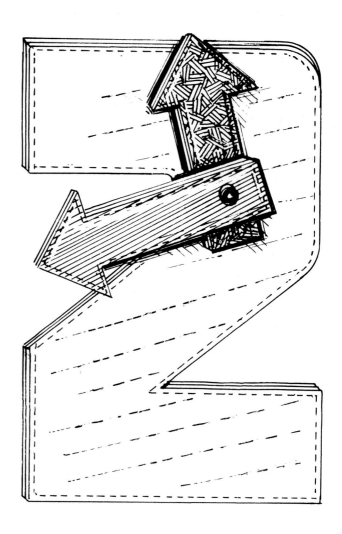

LIGHTS

Top, Middle, Bottom

Lift the covers of the traffic light to reveal the colors of the top, middle, and bottom lights.

Discuss

- Things with a *top, middle,* and *bottom*: Christmas tree—top star, ornaments, tree stand; person—head, belly button, feet; birthday cake—candles, cake, dish
- Things that light up—television, lightning bug, neon signs, flashlight, video games
- Things that come in threes—clover leaves, twisted pretzel loops, triangle sides, tricycle wheels, "three strikes and you're out"

Things to Do

- Study a real traffic light.
- Count the number of traffic lights on a trip.
- Recite the nursery rhymes "Three Little Kittens" and "Rub-a-Dub-Dub."
- Read the stories "Goldilocks and the Three Bears" and "The Three Little Pigs."
- Sing the song "Three Blind Mice."
- Make a **YES & NO sign.**
  1. Cut out a red and a green paper circle to fit on a white paper plate.
  2. Paste a circle to each side of the plate.
  3. Staple on a cardboard handle.
  4. The green side (GO) answers a question with *yes,* the red side

Instructions

NUMBER PAGE

1. **Patterns**—Make the traffic light 4 × 6½ inches (10 × 16.25 cm), and the lights and covers 2-inch (5-cm) circles. Make the side visors 1½ inches (3.75 cm) long. Trace the number *3*.
2. Using the patterns, cut out appliqués from felt. Cut out one red, one amber, and one green circle. Cut out three covers and six visors. Also cut out a cap for the traffic light.
3. Sew the colored circles in a row, centered on the traffic light. Sew a cover over each colored circle, across the top.
4. Pin the appliqués, with the visors tucked under the sides of the traffic light, on the page, and sew them in place.
5. Print the words "LIGHTS," "Top," "Middle," and "Bottom" with fabric paints. Draw decorative details.

NUMBER TOY

1. Draw a large *3* on paper for the pattern.
2. Using the pattern, cut out two felt numbers. Also cut out a red, an amber, a green, and three white circles.
3. Add an appliqué or painted heart (red), star (yellow), and clover (green) on the white circles.
4. Sew the white circles on the three arms of a number, with the heart on the top and the clover on the bottom.
5. Sew the colored circles over their corresponding color designs.
6. Sew the numbers together with a little stuffing between them.

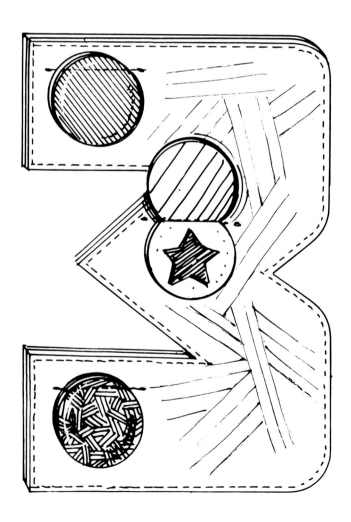

3 LIGHTS
Top · Middle · Bottom

LEGS

On, Under

The cat can sit on or under the table.

Discuss

- Things placed *on* a table—tablecloth, spoons, dishes, flowers, glasses, food; things found *under* a table—chair legs, feet, carpet, crumbs, dog
- Things that come in fours—seasons, four-leaf clover, car tires, major points of a compass, four-sided pyramid, animal's legs
- Big cat cousins—lion, tiger, leopard, cheetah, puma

Things to Do

- Adopt a cat from an animal shelter.
- Befriend a cat.
- Help set the table.
- Collect a bouquet of wild flowers for the breakfast table.
- Turn a table into a playhouse by placing a sheet over it.
- Make a **lucky charm dessert.**
  1. Make a four-leaf clover on a dessert plate with four slices of kiwifruit. Add a stem of raisins.
  2. Pour enough lime gelatin dessert to cover the fruit. Refrigerate.

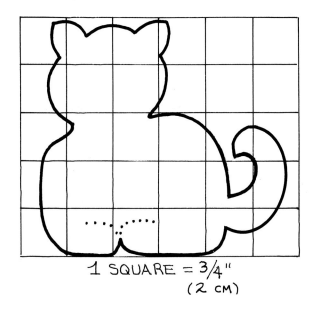

1 SQUARE = 3/4"
(2 CM)

NUMBER TOY

1. Draw a large 4 with an extended crossbar on paper for the pattern.
2. Using the pattern, cut two felt numbers. Also cut out a simple Cheshire cat head.
3. Make a cat face on one head and sew self-fastening tape to the other, before sewing both together.
4. Sew self-fastening tape on the top right and bottom left of the number's crossbar.
5. Sew the numbers together with a little stuffing between them.

Instructions

NUMBER PAGE

1. **Patterns**—Enlarge the cat on the grid (1 square = ¾ inch or 1.87 cm). (See "Grids," p. 8.) Make the tabletop from a 3 × 7-inch (7.5 × 17.5-cm) rectangle with the short sides cut on angles. Trace number 4.
2. Using the patterns, cut appliqués from felt. Cut two cats. Also cut out four legs, two shorter than the others, a vase, and flowers.
3. To construct the cat (see "Independent Appliqués," p. 10), add a face and bow on one cat and self-fastening tape on the other, before sewing the two together.
4. Pin the remaining appliqués on a page and sew them in place.
5. Sew self-fastening tape on and under the table.
6. Print the words "LEGS," "On," and "Under" with fabric paints. Draw decorative details.

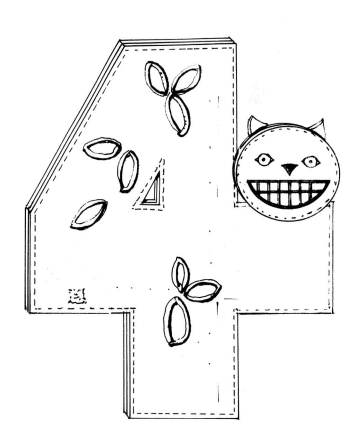

POINTS

Upside Down, Right Side Up

Turn the starfish upside down to see its other face.

Discuss

- Things that turn *upside down*—hourglass, bats, stunt airplanes, you
- Creatures that live on the bottom of the ocean—lobsters, clams, crabs, sea urchins, oysters, coral
- A musical ensemble called a quintet
- Stars in the sky
- Things that come in *fives*—fingers on a hand (counting the thumb), toes on each foot, toenails on one foot, sides of a pentagon, lines of a music staff

Things to Do

- Play "This Little Piggy" on your toes.
- Photocopy an outline of a star many times, and color it in with fanciful designs.
- In an atlas, find flags of countries that have stars in their designs.
- Hang drawings upside down.
- Help make a pineapple upside-down cake.
- Create a **starry night.**
  1. Make a star pattern, following directions below.
  2. Cut many stars from aluminum foil or white paper.
  3. Tie a short piece of string to each star.
  4. Hang the stars on long strings that crisscross the room near the ceiling.

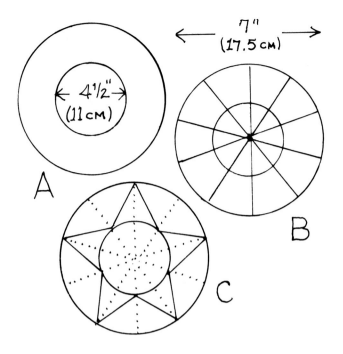

A

B

C

4½" (11 cm)

7" (17.5 cm)

5. Print the words "POINTS," "Upside Down," and "Right Side Up" with fabric paints. Draw a face on the starfish with a curved line (smiling mouth) above and below the eyes. Paint bubbles and add spangles.

NUMBER TOY

1. Draw a large 5 on paper for the pattern.
2. Using the pattern, cut out two felt numbers. Also cut out two faces.
3. Sew or glue a face on the top and bottom (upside down) of one number.
4. Sew the numbers together with a little stuffing between them.

Instructions

NUMBER PAGE

1. **Patterns**—Cut a 7-inch (17.5-cm) free-form star, or for a more accurate star, follow diagrams A, B, and C as shown. Trace number 5.
2. Using the patterns, cut appliqués from felt. Cut out two stars. Trim the star pattern and cut out a smaller third star. Also cut out scalloped seashells.
3. To construct the starfish (see "Independent Appliqués," p. 10), sew the small star on one large star, and sew self-fastening tape on the other. Sew the stars together; add a rickrack border.
4. Sew self-fastening tape on the page in the spot where you want to place starfish. Sew on the remaining appliqués.

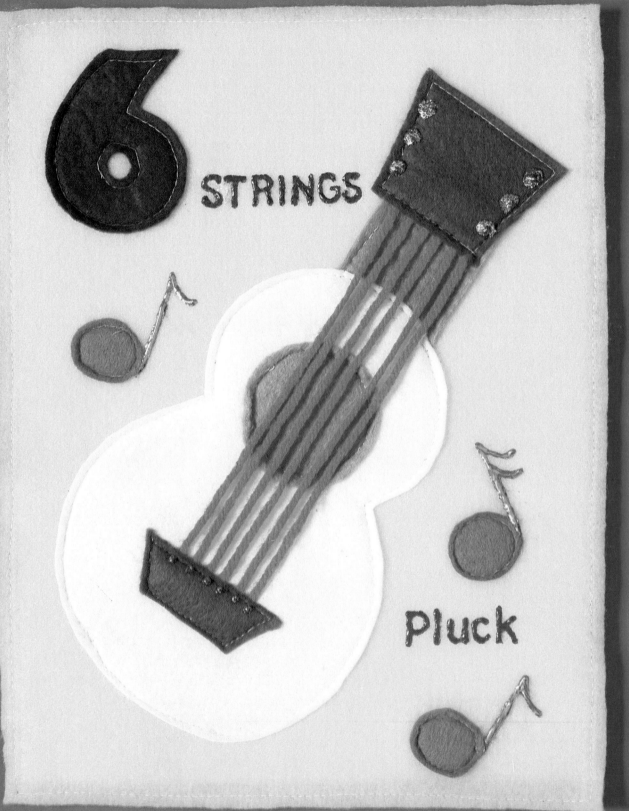

STRINGS

Pluck

Gently pluck the strings.

Discuss

- Things that are *plucked*—chicken feathers, string instruments, fruit from a bowl
- String instruments—violin, viola, banjo, zither, balalaika, piano, harp
- Things that come in sixes—half-dozen doughnuts, colors of the rainbow, arms of a snowflake, sides of a hexagon, insect legs
- Favorite songs

Things to Do

- Read Edward Lear's poem "The Owl and the Pussy-Cat."
- Recite the nursery rhyme "Sing a Song of Sixpence."
- Listen to popular music and try to recognize the guitar.
- Visit a music store.
- Create **lacy snowflakes.**
  1. Trace around a dish on paper and cut out the circle.
  2. Fold the circle in half. Fold the half into three equal sections. Fold it in half one more time.
  3. Cut away a corner of the curved edge of the folded paper to form a point.
  4. Cut out shapes along both folded sides.
  5. Open the paper.

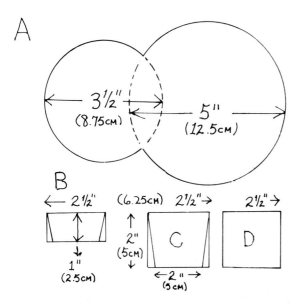

A

$3\frac{1}{2}''$ (8.75cm) $5''$ (12.5cm)

B

← $2\frac{1}{2}''$ (6.25cm) $2\frac{1}{2}''$ → $2\frac{1}{2}''$ →

2" (5cm)   C   D

1" (2.5cm)   ← 2" → (5cm)

Instructions

NUMBER PAGE

1. **Patterns**—Draw the guitar (A), the bridge (B), the head (C), and the neck (D) to the dimensions given. Trace number *6*.
2. Using the patterns, cut out appliqués from felt. Also cut out notes and a 2-inch (5-cm) circle for the sound hole.
3. Sew the sound hole on the top half of the guitar.
4. Pin the appliqués, except the head and bridge, on the page with the neck tucked under the guitar. Sew them in place.
5. Pin the bridge on the lower half of the guitar, with the ends of six equally spaced lengths of yarn tucked under it. Sew it in place.
6. Pin the head to the top of the neck.
7. Extend the yarn across the guitar, and tuck the ends under the head after the excess has been trimmed away. Sew in place.

8. Print the words "STRINGS" and "Pluck" with fabric paints. Add six keys on the head and six pegs on the bridge with large dots of paint. Draw stems and flags on the notes.

NUMBER TOY

1. Draw a large *6* on paper for a pattern.
2. Using the pattern, cut out two felt numbers.
3. Sew the numbers together with a little stuffing between them.
4. Punch an equal number of holes on opposite sides of the number's opening.
5. Feed yarn in and out of the holes. Hide the knotted ends on the underside.

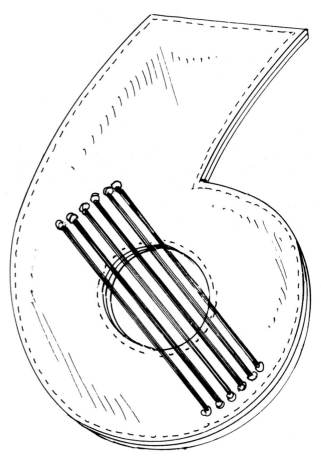

DAYS

Puzzle

Fit the puzzle pieces together in the order of the days of the week.

Discuss

- Things put together like a *puzzle*— words in a board game, ingredients in a recipe, designs in a quilt, jigsaw pieces in a puzzle
- Weekday things to do and weekend things to do
- Days of the week this year's holidays fall on

Things to Do

- On a special calendar, mark off each day that passes with a sticker, rubber stamp, or crayon design.
- Read the tale "Snow White and the Seven Dwarfs."
- Count the points on the Statue of Liberty's crown.
- Create your own **puzzle.**
  1. Draw a design on paper with crayons.
  2. Cut the paper into seven parts. They can be seven equal rectangles, or seven nondescript shapes.

Instructions

NUMBER PAGE

1. **Patterns**—Divide a 7-inch (17.5-cm) circle into seven equal wedges. Draw a second circle 6½ inches (16.25 cm). Trace the number 7.
2. Using the patterns, cut out appliqués from felt. Cut two of each wedge from a different color.
3. To construct the wedges (see "Independent Appliqués," p. 10), sew self-fastening tape to one of each two wedges, before sewing the two together.
4. Pin the remaining appliqués on the page and sew them in place.
5. Sew self-fastening tape on the circle to match the tape on the wedges.
6. Print the words "DAYS," "Puzzle," and "1 WEEK" (in the middle of the circle) with fabric paints. Write the initials or abbreviations of the days of the week on the wedges. Draw decorative details, as you wish.

NUMBER TOY

1. Draw a large 7 on paper for the pattern.
2. Using the pattern, cut out two felt numbers. Also cut out a small oval.
3. Sew seven pieces of self-fastening tape equally spaced along the right side of one number.
4. Sew the numbers together with a little stuffing between them.
5. Sew self-fastening tape to the oval.
6. Write the days of the week with fabric paint on the number toy, in line with the tape. Draw a happy face on the oval. Move the happy face to each new day of the week.

TENTACLES

Overlap

Overlap the octopus's tentacles.

Discuss

- Things that *overlap* other things—fish scales, rose petals, bird feathers, cabbage leaves, pinecone scales
- Octopus "ink"
- Other sea creatures with tentacles—squid, jellyfish, cuttlefish
- What you'll be doing when you're eight years old

Things to Do

- Draw colorful shapes on paper, each overlapping the other a little.
- Read a book on sea creatures.
- Draw a smiling sun with eight shining rays.
- Ice-skate figure eights.
- Create **butterfly eights.**
  1. On paper, draw large and small *8*'s on their sides for butterfly wings.
  2. Color in bodies and antennas.
  3. Color in wing designs.

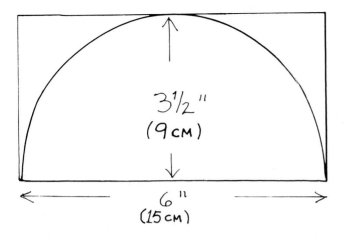

3½" (9cm)

6" (15cm)

NUMBER TOY

1. Draw a large *8* on paper for the pattern.
2. Using the pattern, cut out two felt numbers.
3. With lengths of yarn tucked inside the toy sew the numbers together with a little stuffing between them.

Instructions

NUMBER PAGE

1. **Patterns**—Draw the octopus to the dimensions given. Trace the number *8*.
2. Using the patterns, cut out appliqués from felt. Also cut out eyes and seaweed.
3. Sew on eyes and add a mouth to the octopus.
4. Pin the appliqués on the page with the ends of eight equal lengths of yarn tucked under the straight edge of the octopus. Sew them in place.
5. Print the words "TENTACLES" and "Overlap" with fabric paints. Add decorative details and spangles.

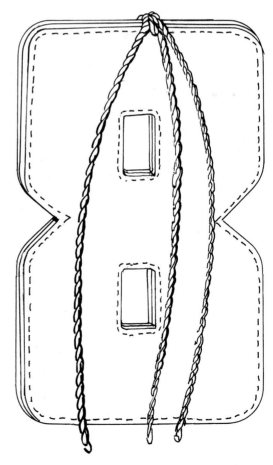

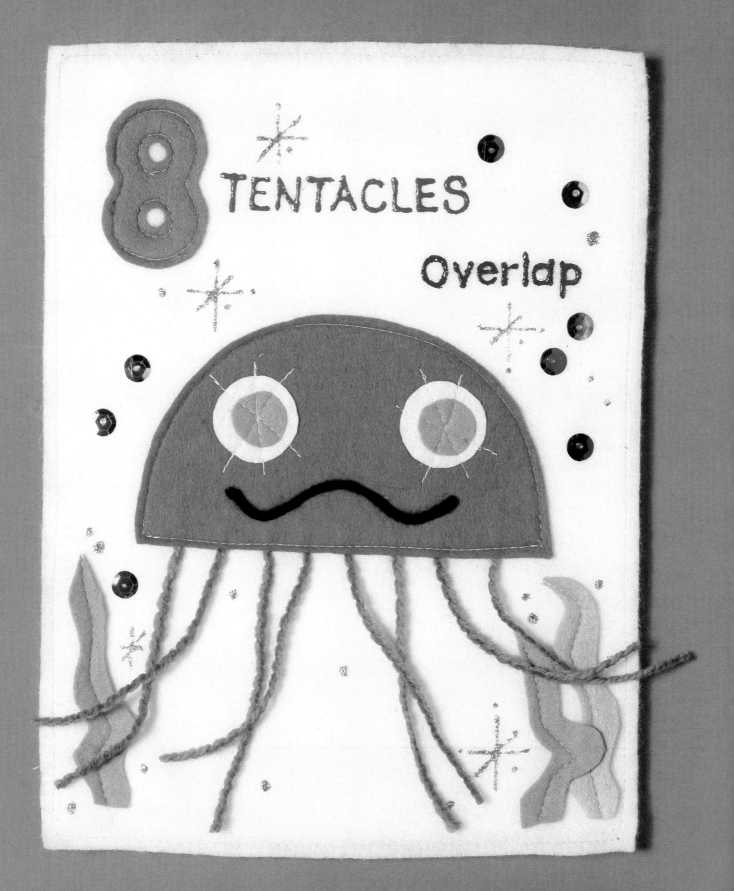

 **VEGETABLES**

Match

VEGETABLES

Match

Match the vegetables with their corresponding shapes in the garden.

Discuss

- Things that *match*—shoes, socks, gloves, earmuffs, jacket sleeves, pant legs
- Favorite vegetables and vegetables you don't like
- Ways to prepare potatoes—bake, French fry, mash, scallop, chip
- The difference between fruits and vegetables

Things to Do

- Dry pumpkin seeds for a healthy snack.
- Grow a tomato plant in a flowerpot.
- Visit a produce store or a vegetable garden.
- Read about Peter Rabbit's adventures in Mr. McGregor's vegetable garden in Beatrix Potter's "The Tale of Peter Rabbit."
- Create a **potato print.**
  1. Cut a potato in half.
  2. Scratch a simple design into the cut side of each half.
  3. Cut away the potato around the design for the background.
  4. Paint the raised design with poster or watercolor paint, and print your design on paper.

Instructions

NUMBER PAGE

1. **Patterns**—Make the garden a 7-inch (17.5-cm) square. Draw small, free-form vegetables and separate greenery. Trace the number *9*.
2. Using the patterns, cut out appliqués from felt. Cut two of each vegetable. From a neutral color, also cut out a smaller matching shape for each.
3. To construct the vegetables (see "Independent Appliqués," p. 10), sew self-fastening tape to one of each two vegetables, before sewing them together with greenery tucked between them.
4. Before sewing the neutral shapes on the garden, sew self-fastening tape to each.
5. Sew the garden and the number on the page.
6. Print the words "VEGETABLES" and "Match" with fabric paints. Draw decorative details.

NUMBER TOY

1. Draw a large *9* on paper for the pattern.
2. Using the pattern, cut out two brown felt numbers. Also cut out small vegetable appliqués.
3. Sew or glue the vegetables on one number.
4. Sew the numbers together with a little stuffing between them.

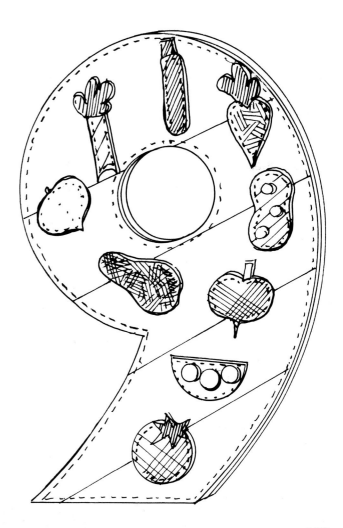

INDEX